Company's Address:
Kaleidoscope Paints Limited,
Chanka Trace,
El Socorro Extension Road,
Churchill Roosevelt Highway,
San Juan,
Trinidad, West Indies

Publisher's Address:
Amazon Kindle Direct Publishing
P.O. Box 81226
Seattle, WA 98108-1226
USA

Kaleidoscope Paints Limited's mission is to be a company recognized worldwide for high-quality products, customer satisfaction, personalized business relationships, employee motivation, and value to its shareholders.

For more information on this company: https://kscopepaints.com/
Email: info@kplgrouptt.com
Telephone: (868) 638-2001, 2213, 2214, 2215, 2216, 2222, 2369, 5183
Fax: (868) 675-0416, 675-2001

© Dr. Joshua A. Jogie 2023

All rights reserved. This book and/or any part thereof shall not be reproduced, distributed, or transmitted in any format and/or by any means whatsoever without prior written authorization and permission from the Author, Kaleidoscope Paints Limited and the Parson family. All requisite permissions have been obtained from the Parson family and Kaleidoscope Paints Limited for the relevant photographs, logos and accounts appearing in this book.

50th Anniversary Edition: First published June 18th, 2023 (Father's Day)

Published by Amazon Kindle Direct Publishing

ISBN 9798395221872 Hardcover (Kaleidoscope Paints Edition)

ISBN 9798399218250 Paperback

Disclaimer

The information contained in this book represents the Author's best efforts to ensure the accuracy and completeness of the facts presented. All events, incidents, and persons depicted herein are based on available documents, personal accounts, and memory recollections. While every precaution has been taken in the preparation of this book, due to the passage of time, the potential for human error, or changes in circumstances, the Author cannot guarantee that every detail aligns with actual historical events or circumstances. The Author, publisher, and anyone involved in the creation and distribution of this work shall not be liable for any errors, discrepancies, or divergences from actual historical occurrences that may be contained within.

Acknowledgements:

Painting a canvas as intimate and comprehensive as this one requires not just research, but also a personal connection. The successful completion of this biography owes much to the support and contributions of numerous individuals.

I would like to extend my deepest gratitude to Monica Parson, the loving wife of the late Stephen Sonny Parson (SSP) and matriarch of the Parson family, "Grams", whose insights, and anecdotes about Stephen's personal life provided a tender, unseen dimension to the book. Her warmth and willingness to share their journey greatly enriched this biography.

To Christine Deyalsingh, Carol Parsan, Ian Parson, Mahindra Deyalsingh, Dale Parson, Rabindranath Jogie, Cindy Parsan-Singh, and Deborah Guppy, your personal reflections on Stephen have provided an invaluable perspective. Your openness in sharing your experiences has allowed a completer and more nuanced portrait of this extraordinary man to be painted.

To Stephen's elder brother, the late Mun Mun Parsan, your insights into Stephen's family have been invaluable in understanding the broader family context in which Stephen's life unfolded. I am profoundly grateful for your contribution.

To Margaret Mohammed and David Khan, your shared memories added depth to the narrative, and I am immensely grateful for your willingness to contribute.

Suzanne Khadoo-Mankee and Donna Durall have also offered their unique perspective and shared delightful tales that added color to this biography. Thank you for your valuable contributions.

To Barry Deyalsingh and Laura Deyalsingh, your stories and reminiscences about SSP have helped to portray the family man behind the successful businessman. Your accounts breathed life into the man I've tried to illustrate through these pages. To Bryan Deyalsingh, Jason Jogie, Nicholas Singh, Jeremy Jogie, and Ritchard Singh, thank you for your assistance with providing interview content.

A special note of gratitude is reserved for Stephen's neighbor, Dianne Ramlakhan, and Stephen's Minister, the late Reverend Cyril Paul; Stephen's close friends and fellow church members. Their shared experiences and perspectives have added another layer of understanding to Stephen's character. The tales of their shared faith and community interactions have shed light on Stephen as a devout church member and compassionate friend. Your contributions have helped to truly bring Stephen's spirit alive in this biography, and for that, I am sincerely grateful.

Finally, I wish to thank the loyal employees of Kaleidoscope Paints Limited: Maxmin Richardson, Roy Pustam, Michael Ramai, Helen Ramlal, and Anisa Mohammed. Your enduring commitment to the company and your personal insights into the man who led you have greatly informed this biography. The experiences you shared underscored the essence of Stephen's leadership and his impact on those around him.

Every single person mentioned here has played a significant part in the painting of this path. To each of you, I extend my heartfelt appreciation for your valuable contribution to the retelling of Stephen Sonny Parson's extraordinary journey.

Thank you.

A Welcoming Message from Monica Parson, wife of Stephen Sonny Parson:

Monica Parson

As the wife of Stephen Sonny Parson, I had the unique pleasure of sharing my life with him, the intimate experiences and beautiful moments that helped shape the man that is the subject of this biography. My journey with him began when we were very young. I was a tender teenager when I first met him, a young man just two (2) to three (3) years older. My mother, a discerning woman, saw in Stephen, a promising future and readily approved of our relationship.

From those early days of youth, our bond was strong and unshaken. We shared an understanding and a companionship that felt natural and right. My love for Stephen, combined with our closeness in age, made the decision to marry him an easy one. His character was compelling: never quarrelsome, always considerate, deeply thoughtful, and very focused on goal achievement. These traits attracted me to him, but they also brought him success in his professional life.

During his early career after we first met, Stephen was recognized for his diligent work ethic, dedication to his job, commitment, and the quality of his output in his workplace. We were brought together by Stephen's generosity, where our families interacted and agreed upon the foundation of our relationship. Stephen was always deeply religious, a virtue that went hand in hand with his intelligence and wisdom.

Although Stephen did not further his education, his ambition, his work ethic, his endless fountain of ideas – these attributes reassured me that he would find his path. And indeed, he did. Despite the many challenges he faced in starting his business, he persevered. He was a caring and loving parent and a supportive husband. As his wife, I never experienced any difficulties with him balancing his professional and family life. He was always present for us, making time for his family even as he nurtured his growing business.

Stephen was respected and admired by many, including my own mother, who recognized his good qualities and fully supported our marriage. Despite his health issues later in life, he displayed resilience and strived to lessen the impact on our family. Even those challenging times have become treasured memories for me.

When Stephen passed away, it was a heartbreaking period for our family. We deeply missed his presence, his wisdom, and his warmth. But his legacy lived on especially, in our children, who inherited his values and moral strength; in the church, where he contributed generously; and of course, in Kaleidoscope Paints Limited, his 'child' that stands as a testament to his hard work, dedication, and ingenuity.

Stephen was not just an extraordinary husband and father, but also a generous benefactor and a deeply religious man. He made regular donations to orphanages by having Christmas treats for them. His legacy continues to inspire and guide us, even after his passing. He was an active member of the community Presbyterian Church and held a close friendship with many members and prominent Minister of the church.

Stephen's life story is filled with virtues we can all learn from – his honesty, his generosity, his dedication to his family, and his strong faith. I want the young and upcoming generations to read this book and understand the man behind the story, to draw inspiration from his journey and to apply his values in their own lives.

As readers delve into this life story, they should understand the humble beginnings Stephen came from. He started off riding a bicycle to work, saved for years to afford a car, and used those same savings to start his company. We lived a simple life in the early years. Stephen was a lover of music, a pastime that brought joy into our everyday life.

It is my hope that this portrayal helps you, the reader, to understand the depth and breadth of Stephen's character. He was a man of resilience and determination, a man of deep faith and compassion, and a man who loved his family dearly. This book is a testament to his life, his achievements, and his legacy. I am incredibly proud to have been a part of his journey and to share it with you today.

Sincerely,

Monica Parson
Wife of Stephen Sonny Parson.

A Greeting from Dale Parson, Managing Director of Kaleidoscope Paints Limited, and son of Stephen Sonny Parson:

Dale Parson

Dear Readers,

As you delve into the life and legacy of my father, Stephen Sonny Parson, it is my honor to share a glimpse into my own journey. Inspired by my father's remarkable entrepreneurial spirit, I am currently serving as the Managing Director of Kaleidoscope Paints Limited, a dynamic, diversified group in the Manufacturing and Distribution Industry, specializing in Paints, Adhesives, and Brewery/Beverage products, exporting throughout the Caribbean, Central America, South America, USA, Canada, and England.

The wishes of my father were for me to become a Medical Doctor after attending Hillview College. However, as he got ill, things changed, and he encouraged me to change my academic direction towards Chemical Engineering. This was so that I could be academically poised to run the paint factory. So, instead of medicine, I pursued a BSc in Engineering from the University of the West Indies (UWI), an accolade that laid a strong foundation for my business acumen. Fueled by the desire to shape strategic decision-making processes, I further earned an MSc in Strategic Leadership and Management from UWI, and then pursued a PhD in Business Administration with specialization in Marketing.

This advanced study offers me a comprehensive understanding of market dynamics, enabling me to drive Kaleidoscope Paints Limited's (KPL) products to a wider audience and expand our reach.

Professional affiliations form an essential part of my career, and I am a proud member of the Board of Engineers of Trinidad and Tobago (BOETT) and the Association of Professional Engineers of Trinidad and Tobago (APETT). These Associations keep me abreast of the latest developments in the engineering field, allowing me to integrate innovative practices into our manufacturing process.

As the Managing Director of a regionally recognized privately owned organization, I have gained extensive knowledge and experience across various facets of business operations. This includes, but is not limited to, manufacturing, competitiveness, international trade, management, international business operations, and strategic planning. It is this wealth of knowledge that I bring to the Trinidad and Tobago Manufacturers' Association (TTMA), offering them a wide-ranging understanding of the manufacturing industry, particularly in strategic planning, trade agreement negotiations, and competitiveness.

Presently, I chair the TTMA's Infrastructure Committee (formerly Transport and Logistics), a position that allows me to delve into the operational dynamics of the transport and logistics sector. Additionally, as the current Vice President at TTMA, I am fortunate to play a role in steering the organization's strategic direction.

My ultimate passion in life is to ensure the longevity of the KPL Group as a firmly established international company for a minimum of the next fifty (50) years. My passion is driven by the fact that my father died at a very young age. He sacrificed his health and life to start KPL. My ambition is to ensure it grows profitably for the many generations who read this biography. I will guide the generations to come on Stephen's principles of hard work, integrity, honesty, and humility, to run the business, so that it continues to live long after I am gone.

As you turn the pages of this book, you will learn about my father's unwavering dedication, his visionary leadership, and his profound impact on all those who had the privilege of knowing him. I trust that his story will serve as an enduring source of inspiration and guidance for budding entrepreneurs and business enthusiasts.

Warm Regards,

Dale Parson
Managing Director, Kaleidoscope Paints Limited.

THE PAINTED PATH: STEPHEN SONNY PARSON'S JOURNEY

DR. JOSHUA A. JOGIE

DEDICATION:

In memory of Stephen Sonny Parson:

It's been in my dreams that we've met, where your presence carries the same warmth and charisma that I've heard so much about. It was there within my dreamscape, beneath the glistening stars outside your home, that you gently nudged me to document your story, to recount the legacy you meticulously weaved for future generations.

While I never had the chance to meet you in this tangible world, your influence has been as profound as it has been transformative. I've walked through the halls of Kaleidoscope Paints Limited, your dream made reality, and I've seen firsthand the tireless sacrifices you made and battles you fought. Through these experiences, I've come to know you - not just as my grandfather, but as a visionary, a creator, a mentor, and above all, a man who dared to dream and had the courage to make those dreams come true.

In the echoes of your legacy, I've never truly felt you were gone. The company you founded stands tall and firm, much like a watchful guardian and grandfather, guiding us, encouraging us to follow your footsteps and forge our own paths. It is a testament to your perseverance and steadfast dedication, a beacon that continues to illuminate the way for those who dare to dream.

I hope, wherever you are, you find this book a worthy reflection of your life and the indomitable spirit that has always characterized you. I wish that you could see the thriving tree your seeds have grown into and feel the gratitude of the generations who stand in the shade of the legacy you left behind.

May you find solace in knowing that your sacrifices have not been in vain, that your dream lives on, and that your story has been told.

May you rest in peace, knowing you've done more than anyone could have asked for. This book is a small token of my immense gratitude, a humble tribute to a life so beautifully lived.

May the pages of this book find its way to you, carrying with it my love and admiration. Happy Father's Day.

Your loving Grandson

"Ladies and gentlemen, I'd like to welcome you all, very warmly, to our humble setting. We have made accommodations for everyone. We've done everything possible to make you comfortable and have provided more than enough for us all to enjoy. I invite you all to feel at home and to partake in the joy of this journey. This will be a brief gathering, so we won't keep you too long. As we gather here, I encourage you all to indulge in everything placed for your enjoyment. They were arranged for the sole purpose of providing you with something to enjoy until the main event. So please feel free to help yourself. Thank you all for being here and for partaking in the delight of this journey. May we all enjoy the moments that lie ahead."

– Stephen Sonny Parson, March 3rd, 1990

Table of Contents

BACKGROUND 1
INTRODUCTION 7
PROLOGUE 13
CHAPTER 1 19
CHAPTER 2 24
CHAPTER 3 29
CHAPTER 4 35
CHAPTER 5 40
CHAPTER 6 46
CHAPTER 7 51
CHAPTER 8 54
CHAPTER 9 58
CHAPTER 10 62
CHAPTER 11 66
CHAPTER 12 71
CHAPTER 13 74
CHAPTER 14 78
CHAPTER 15 81
CHAPTER 16 85
CHAPTER 17 88
CHAPTER 18 92
CHAPTER 19 98
CHAPTER 20 106
CHAPTER 21 116
CHAPTER 22 133
CHAPTER 23 137
CHAPTER 24 150
CHAPTER 25 161
CHAPTER 26 166
CHAPTER 27 176
CHAPTER 28 188
CHAPTER 29 197
CHAPTER 30 203
EPILOGUE 211

Background

Laying the Groundwork: Core Principles of Entrepreneurship and Paint Manufacturing

"Success is Not Final, Failure is Not Fatal: it is the Courage to Continue that Counts." – Winston Churchill

Entrepreneurship, at its very core, can be likened to a vibrant dance: it requires balance, creativity, agility, and a profound sense of timing. Much like dancers learning the essential moves before they create their unique choreography, aspiring entrepreneurs must comprehend fundamental principles before embarking on their journeys.

The magic of manufacturing is akin to a grand performance - a symphony of raw materials, machinery, human skills, and innovative processes. Let us dive into the riveting world of entrepreneurship as well as paint manufacturing and familiarize ourselves with its key concepts, keeping in mind the unique socio-economic milieu of Trinidad and Tobago during the mid to late 20th century.

Firstly, entrepreneurship is about taking risks. The future is always uncertain, but entrepreneurs embrace this uncertainty, make calculated decisions, and often venture into uncharted territories. Take for instance the risk Trinidad and Tobago took by diversifying its economy from sugar to oil in the 1970s. This daring shift led to an economic boom, proving that the right kind of risks can lead to enormous rewards.

Secondly, entrepreneurs are problem solvers. They identify gaps in the market and innovate to fill them, essentially turning challenges into opportunities. Think about how many Trinidadian businesses had to adapt during the oil boom era, shifting their focus to serve the changing needs of a more affluent society. Their innovative solutions were the steppingstones to their success.

Thirdly, entrepreneurs are continuous learners. They glean insights from every experience, good or bad, constantly evolving to better meet the needs of their market. They understand that learning is a lifelong journey. For instance, the advent of Trinidad and Tobago's national steelpan instrument is an excellent testament to this principle, the result of the learnings from numerous trials and tribulations faced. The steelpan was born out of necessity and resourcefulness during the war when traditional musical instruments were scarce, reflecting the spirit of innovation and adaptability.

The fourth principle revolves around strategic thinking. Entrepreneurs have a knack for making smart decisions to position their business advantageously. Strategic planning was key for businesses during the period of economic transition in Trinidad and Tobago when businesses had to readjust their strategies to cater to an economy now dominated by the oil industry.

The fifth principle of entrepreneurship centers on the 'people first' approach. Successful entrepreneurs value their teams and foster an inclusive environment where everyone's contributions matter. During the civil rights movements of the 1970s, Trinidad and Tobago saw a shift in business cultures, with companies increasingly recognizing the importance of a diverse and engaged workforce.

In summation, entrepreneurship is a multifaceted discipline that requires an understanding of risk-taking, problem-solving, lifelong learning, strategic planning, the 'people first' approach, and customer engagement. In essence, entrepreneurship is about creating value in innovative ways, which, as we have seen, is a timeless principle that resonates regardless of the socio-economic climate or geographical location.

Manufacturing, in its simplest definition, is the transformation of raw materials into finished goods. This transformation journey consists of three core stages: acquiring raw materials, processing these materials, and delivering the final product. Each stage requires precision, expertise, and an understanding of how individual components work together.

Paint manufacturing is an exquisite example of this symphony in action, weaving together science, artistry, and the demands of the marketplace. The process starts with the acquisition of raw materials, primarily pigments, resins, solvents, and additives.

Pigments provide color and opacity, making the paint visually appealing and also aids in ensuring that it adequately covers the surface. The primary pigment in most paints is titanium dioxide, a white pigment widely found in Trinidad and Tobago's local mineral resources during the late 20th century.

Resins, or binders, hold the pigment particles together and provide adhesion to the surface. In the Trinidadian context, acrylic resins were commonly used due to their durability and resistance to the tropical climate's moisture and sunlight.

Solvents keep the paint in a liquid state until application, after which they evaporate, leaving behind a solid, dry paint film. Water-based paints, increasingly popular for their environmental friendliness, utilize water as the primary solvent.

Finally, additives enhance the properties of the paint, such as its flow, drying time, and resistance to mold and fungus - critical aspects in a humid, tropical environment like Trinidad and Tobago.

Once these raw materials are gathered, the manufacturing process can begin, typically divided into three primary stages: premixing, milling, and let-down.

During premixing, pigments are mixed with some solvents and additives to form a smooth paste. The milling stage then follows, in which the pigment paste is ground to break down the pigment particles into smaller sizes. This grinding also ensures a better dispersion of pigments throughout the paint, leading to a more uniform and stable product.

The final stage, let-down, involves blending the milled pigment dispersion with the remaining components, including the binder and additional solvents or water. The result is a well-mixed paint that is then filtered to remove any remaining lumps or foreign materials, ready for packaging and distribution.

This overview of manufacturing and the production of paints sets the stage for a deep exploration of one of the most vibrant industries in Trinidad and Tobago during the late 20th century. With these foundational aspects in mind, we will be better equipped to appreciate the extraordinary fusion of entrepreneurship and paint manufacturing that unfolded during the pivotal years of change in Trinidad and Tobago – a change that will be unfolded and demystified through the pages of this book.

Overview:

The Background, "Laying the Groundwork: Core Principles of Entrepreneurship and Paint Manufacturing", can be likened to a vibrant dance: it requires balance, creativity, agility, and a profound sense of timing. This chapter explores the fundamental principles of entrepreneurship and the manufacturing industry, with a focus on the unique socio-economic milieu of Trinidad and Tobago during the mid to late 20th century. It highlights the principles of risk-taking, problem-solving, continuous learning, strategic thinking, the 'people first' approach, and customer engagement. The chapter then delves into the world of paint manufacturing, explaining the stages involved in transforming raw materials into finished goods. By understanding these foundational aspects, readers will gain a deeper appreciation for the entrepreneurial and manufacturing journeys that unfolded in Trinidad and Tobago during this transformative period.

Key Points:

1. Entrepreneurship requires risk-taking, calculated decisions, and the willingness to venture into uncharted territories.
2. Entrepreneurs are problem solvers who turn challenges into opportunities and innovate to fill gaps in the market.
3. Continuous learning is essential for entrepreneurs, and they glean insights from every experience to better meet market needs.
4. Strategic thinking allows entrepreneurs to make smart decisions that position their businesses advantageously.
5. Entrepreneurs prioritize a 'people first' approach, valuing their teams and fostering an inclusive environment.

6. Customer engagement is crucial, and entrepreneurs strive to understand and meet their clients' wants, needs, and expectations.
7. The manufacturing process involves acquiring raw materials, processing them, and delivering the final product.
8. Paint manufacturing exemplifies the integration of science, artistry, and market demands.
9. Raw materials in paint manufacturing include pigments, resins, solvents, and additives.
10. The manufacturing process consists of premixing, milling, and let-down stages to achieve a well-mixed paint ready for packaging and distribution.

INTRODUCTION

A JOURNEY ACROSS SEAS: PARSAN'S VOYAGE AND ITS LEGACY

"You take a capsule from India, leave it here for a hundred years, and this is what you get." - Mungal Patasar

Our tale begins by tracing the ancestral roots of Stephen Sonny Parson. His lineage can be traced back to the humble village named Khojari, tucked away under the 'thana' (police station) of Chiraiakote, in the district of Azamgarh of the Uttar Pradesh state, India. In 1896, a single parent family of three, led by Stephen's grandmother, Bachni, embarked on a voyage seeking fortune in distant lands. Accompanying her were her two young sons, eight-year-old Parsotum and four-year-old Parsan, the latter being Stephen's father.

Historically, in India, upon the death of a woman's husband, widows were expected to sacrifice their lives by joining their deceased husbands in their funeral pyres, through the practice of "sati", or else the grieving widow became a societal outcast. This terrifying prospect led Parsan's mother to seek a new beginning for her family in distant Trinidad. This trans-oceanic passage was arduous, but served as the chance at a fresh start, away from the oppressive social norms which made the journey worthwhile.

Bachni, the daughter of Pahlad, was a strong-willed woman of thirty (30) years. She found herself standing at the precipice of a profound decision. Her husband, Jhaboo, was absent from their life-changing voyage, an absence so resounding that the field on Bachni's immigration documents for a spouse was conspicuously left blank, underscoring the depth of her courage and determination to embark on this journey with her two young sons alone.

On May 15th, 1896, this family of three was registered at the sub-depot of Ghazipur. They then journeyed to the bustling city of Calcutta, a hub of colonial activity, where they were medically and mentally examined in preparation for emigration to Trinidad. Along with six hundred and forty (640) fellow Indians, they boarded the Erne sailing ship on August 4th, 1896, a tremendous and hazardous journey that would significantly shape the destiny of the future Parsons.

This ship carried them across the dark waters of three oceans to Trinidad, a voyage that cost seven of their ship companions their lives. From the sprawling vistas of India to the verdant shores of the small West Indian Island of Trinidad, Parsan's story is as much about a personal journey as it is about a historical shift that molded generations, including Stephen himself.

The adventurous family disembarked the Erne at Nelson Island immigration depot of Trinidad on November 12th, 1896, after a long, arduous voyage of one hundred and one (101) days. Here, Bachni and her sons were assigned to the Aranguez Estate for their indentureship. This marked the beginning of their new life, with the cultural richness of India firmly embedded in their hearts, shaping the future of their generations.

Indentureship, the system of bonded labor, was a significant factor in the history of Trinidad and Tobago during the late 19th and early 20th centuries. According to General Register K for Indian Indentured Laborers, the Grecian, Main, Erne, Avone and Rhine were the vessels that brought Parsan along with three thousand and twenty-three (3,023) Indians to Trinidad in 1896. Their story, like that of many others, is a testament to the courage and resilience of the Indian diaspora.

Indentureship, despite its years of hardships and sacrifices, created a melting pot of cultures in Trinidad and Tobago. Parsan and other indentured laborers brought with them, among other things, their traditions, language, and values. For Parsan, the Hindi language was a link to the motherland, a reminder of a heritage rooted in India's fertile soils. However, with time, English, the language of their new home, became their primary means of communication, demonstrating the cultural adaptation that often accompanies immigration. He began his life in Trinidad as a young boy under this system of indentureship. The trials and tribulations he experienced instilled a spirit of resilience and grit that would significantly shape the destiny of the Parsons, including Stephen himself.

Over the years, Parsan, and other indentured laborers like him, sowed the seeds of their culture in Trinidad. Despite the hardships, Parsan made Trinidad his home. Instead of returning to India at the end of his indentureship, Parsan chose to lay roots in Trinidad, working hard to secure properties that would be passed on to his progeny, eventually settling with his family along the bustling Eastern Main Road, Trinidad. This legacy of perseverance, resourcefulness, and foresight undoubtedly had a profound impact on Stephen, shaping his entrepreneurial spirit which will later become acutely evident.

Creating a life for himself in Trinidad, Parsan married Sancharie from Las Lomas, and together they parented a large family. His children, each unique and resilient in their own right, carried forward his legacy. Among them was his fourteenth child, a son with a spirit as formidable as his father's, named Stephen, whose life and achievements we delve into as this tale unfolds.

The genealogical narrative of the Parson family, in line with Trinidadian tradition, bears an interesting twist. At one juncture, Parsan, Stephen's father, chose to adopt 'Ram' as his last name, thus being known as Parsan Ram. Following local custom during that era, Stephen and his siblings adopted their father's first name, 'Parsan', as their surname. This practice was commonplace in Trinidad, exemplifying the familial ties and cultural norms that characterized the society during that period. Stephen's original surname, Parsan, thus mirrored the rich cultural tapestry of his time, preserving the legacy of his father and rooting his identity firmly within the familial lineage and traditions of his homeland.

Stephen Sonny Parson was the youngest in his family and he even had nephews and nieces who were older than him. This unique position within the family structure, along with the rich heritage brought by Parsan, undoubtedly shaped Stephen's worldview.

Parsan's religious traditions, integral to his Indian identity, remained a significant part of Stephen's life. As Hindus, annual religious prayers and pujas marked their years. When Stephen converted to Presbyterianism after marriage, he still maintained ties with his Hindu roots, especially during times of illness when he sought comfort and strength in the rituals of his ancestors.

Today, Stephen's family continues to honor these traditions, a testament to the enduring influence of their Indian heritage. Parsan's voyage and his life in Trinidad, as an indentured laborer and a property owner, is a story of resilience, adaptability, and determination, traits that were mirrored in Stephen's own life and business ventures.

In examining Stephen's journey, we must not forget this rich tapestry of cultural heritage and historical context that shaped him. Understanding this connection, as Parsan's journey from an indentured laborer to a property owner, provides a deeper insight into Stephen's entrepreneurial spirit and the legacy he left behind. This is not just the story of a man; it's the story of a lineage that crossed seas and defied norms to create their destiny.

Overview:

Our tale begins with Parsan, the father of Stephen Sonny Parson, whose journey from India to Trinidad in 1896 significantly shaped the destiny of the Parson family, including Stephen himself. The chapter explores the historical context of indentureship, a system of bonded labor, and the courage and resilience of the Indian diaspora. Parsan's decision to seek a new beginning in Trinidad and his subsequent settlement became the foundation of Stephen's entrepreneurial spirit. The chapter also highlights the cultural heritage and religious traditions that were passed down through generations, ultimately shaping Stephen's worldview and leaving a lasting impact on his life and business ventures.

Key Points:

1. Parsan's journey from India to Trinidad during the era of indentureship shaped the destiny of the Parson family, including Stephen Sonny Parson.
2. Indentureship was a system of bonded labor that brought indentured laborers from India to Trinidad and Tobago.
3. Parsan's mother's desire to escape the oppressive social norms in India led the family to embark on the arduous journey to Trinidad.
4. The indentured laborers brought with them their traditions, language, and values, creating a cultural melting pot in Trinidad and Tobago.
5. Parsan's decision to lay roots in Trinidad instead of returning to India at the end of his indentureship demonstrated perseverance, resourcefulness, and foresight.
6. Stephen Sonny Parson's unique position in the family and the rich heritage brought by Parsan shaped his worldview.

7. Parsan's religious traditions remained a significant part of Stephen's life, even after his conversion to Presbyterianism.
8. The enduring influence of their Indian heritage is reflected in the continuation of traditions by Stephen's family today.
9. Understanding the historical context and cultural heritage provides deeper insights into Stephen's entrepreneurial spirit and the legacy he left behind.
10. Parsan's journey from an indentured laborer to a property owner represents resilience, adaptability, and determination that mirrored Stephen's life and business ventures.

Prologue

Early Years and Family Life

"You cannot know where you're going unless you know where you've come from." – Derek Walcott

Born on the sunny island of Trinidad on December 8th, 1935, Stephen Sonny Parson was one among a vibrant family of fourteen (14) children. His father migrated to Trinidad from India and eventually became an indentured laborer. The Parson's family home, nestled along the bustling Eastern Main Road, was a mélange of laughter, shared dreams, and the unfettered spirit of unity. Within these lively quarters, Stephen grew up within a family of ten brothers, including himself as the youngest sibling, and four sisters, learning the values of hard work, perseverance, and mutual respect.

The Parson's means of survival were as humble as their abode. The family reared cows and planted crops, a task that required dedication and labor, serving as a foundation for Stephen's strong work ethic. Transport was facilitated by a sturdy donkey cart, a testament to their modest living but resilience in the face of adversity. Parsan, Stephen's father, though not known for his overt involvement in the family's everyday life, displayed a soft spot for his grandchildren, regularly surprising them with small monetary gifts and affection. This trait, unbeknownst to him, would later be mirrored by Stephen in his own acts of generosity and kindness.

Stephen's upbringing was marked by the coexistence of a tight-knit family dynamic and an ingrained respect for labor. The values imparted to him during these formative years - tenacity, brotherhood, and generosity - would shape his outlook in the years to come, influencing his decisions both in his personal life and his career.

As he bloomed into young adulthood, Stephen harbored dreams of becoming a doctor. He even contemplated an ambitious move to England for further studies in medicine, a testament to his aspiration for knowledge and improvement. However, a twist of fate rerouted his journey when he found love, at the age of twenty (20), and married Monica, at the age of eighteen (18), on September 1st, 1956. Stephen's wife, Monica, described his attractive features as being handsome, charming, educated, ambitious, straight-forward, hardworking, loving, caring, romantic and even mentioned their minimal age difference. His presence was illustrated positively, without any conflict or arguments, a testament to his dedication to his wife's well-being.

With their marriage, Stephen assumed responsibility for his wife's six stepsiblings as well as their eventual six children. At the age of twenty-two (22) years, he welcomed his first child into the world. A year later, at twenty-three (23) years old, Stephen's family expanded with the birth of his second child. At twenty-five (25) years of age, Stephen joyfully welcomed his third child, solidifying his growing lineage. A year later, when Stephen was twenty-six (26), his family blossomed further with the birth of his fourth child. Stephen, a mature man of thirty-one (31), rejoiced as his family grew with the arrival of his fifth child. Finally, when Stephen was thirty-three (33) years old, he celebrated the birth of his sixth child, encapsulating his journey from a young man to a proud father of six wonderful children: four (4) girls and two (2) boys.

Displaying immense adaptability and willingness to sacrifice personal dreams for the greater good, Stephen put his aspirations of being a doctor aside. In this crucial phase of his life, he stepped into the paint industry, a decision that would dramatically alter his life and leave an unforgettable mark on the commercial landscape of Trinidad and Tobago.

Stephen's professional journey commenced at British Paints (Caribbean) Limited in 1955, with humble beginnings where he would commute to work on his bicycle. Stephen's hard work and dedication to his job and his family over the years allowed him to purchase a car as well as a new home for his large family.

In the span of a few formative years, Stephen was faced with the profound loss of his parents; when Stephen was twenty-four (24), his mother, Sancharie, passed away on January 7th, 1959, and his father, Parsan, followed on August 6th, 1965. Stephen was thirty (30) years old at the time of his father's passing, a young man navigating the complexities of adulthood amidst these significant personal losses.

With the eventual merging of British Paints (Caribbean) Limited with Berger Paints Trinidad Limited in 1969, Stephen honed his skills in the business and gained a fundamental understanding of raw materials and the quality, and its importance in making quality paint products, especially under the tutelage of an esteemed British Paints expert. Despite the acquisition of expertise, he felt stifled by the lack of room for growth and job security in this corporate environment. This sense of constraint sparked a flame within Stephen - a flame that would eventually guide him towards the path of entrepreneurship.

From humble beginnings, Stephen Sonny Parson began his ascent, shaping his journey with the qualities instilled in him from his early family life. His tale is a testament to the impact of familial bonds, early life experiences, and the enduring values they propagate. As a child, he was nurtured in an environment of camaraderie, labor, and affection, lessons that he would carry forward into his own family life, his career, and ultimately, his legacy.

Overview:

In the prologue, Sonny Parson's upbringing in Trinidad is highlighted. Born into a vibrant and close-knit family, Stephen learned the values of hard work, perseverance, and unity from his thirteen (13) siblings. Their modest living and reliance on farming and a donkey cart for transportation instilled in him a strong work ethic and resilience. Stephen's father, though not actively involved, displayed generosity towards his grandchildren, a trait that would be reflected in Stephen's own acts of kindness. These formative years shaped Stephen's character, emphasizing tenacity, brotherhood, and generosity, which would influence his personal and professional decisions.

Key Points:

1. Stephen Sonny Parson grew up in a tight-knit family in Trinidad, learning the values of hard work, perseverance, and unity.
2. The family's means of survival involved farming and relying on a donkey cart for transportation.
3. Stephen's father displayed generosity towards his grandchildren, inspiring Stephen's own acts of kindness.
4. Stephen harbored dreams of becoming a doctor but put his aspirations aside after marrying Monica and assuming responsibility for her siblings and their six children.
5. Stephen began his professional journey at British Paints (Caribbean) Limited and later honed his skills in the paint industry after the merger with Berger Paints Trinidad Limited.
6. Despite gaining expertise, Stephen felt constrained by the lack of growth and job security in the corporate environment, which ignited his entrepreneurial spirit.

Below is a table presenting key information related to Stephen Sonny Parson's early years and family life:

Key Information	Details
Birthdate	December 8th, 1935
Family Size	Thirteen (13) siblings
Means of Survival	Farming, rearing cows, planting crops
Transportation	Relied on a donkey cart
Father's Involvement	Displayed generosity towards grandchildren
Stephen's Aspirations	Initially aimed to become a doctor
Marriage and Responsibilities	Married Monica and assumed responsibility for her siblings and six children
Professional Journey	Started at British Paints (Caribbean) Limited
Merger with Berger Paints Trinidad Limited	Honed skills in the paint industry
Constraints and Entrepreneurial Flame	Felt limited growth and job security in the corporate environment, sparking his entrepreneurial spirit

Chapter 1

The Humble Beginnings

"Nothing is impossible. With the right attitude, you can conquer anything." – Ato Boldon

Born into the vibrant culture of Trinidad, Stephen Sonny Parson's life was always destined to mirror the colorful world around him. In 1955, he joined British Paints (Caribbean) Limited, marking the inception of a lifelong relationship with the paint industry. Despite his humble beginnings as a novice, Parson exhibited a unique tenacity and work ethic that propelled him up the ranks.

By 1969, he had become the Administrative Assistant to the Chairman and Managing Director of the British Paints Caribbean Group of Companies. His time at British Paints and his work experience and significant relationships with esteemed experts there, instilled an acute understanding of the business dynamics in the paint industry. This included an expertise and understanding of invaluable management skills, typing and shorthand skills, paint manufacturing as well as raw materials and their importance in quality, shaping his future entrepreneurial vision.

Stephen's early journey shows how perseverance and dedication can facilitate professional growth. His ascension to an administrative position within the organization mirrors the modern trend of organic growth in startups and emphasizes the importance of understanding the ins and outs of an industry before embarking on an entrepreneurial venture.

His keen eye for opportunity was evident when the landscape of his professional life changed unexpectedly. In 1969, British Paints, UK, sold its worldwide operations to an American Chemical Company. Pursuant to this sale, British Paints (Caribbean) Limited was merged with Berger Paints. Unfortunately, this merger resulted in the displacement of numerous personnel, including those at senior levels. The shift in control and the subsequent volatility in his professional environment led Stephen to consider new avenues, demonstrating his resilience and adaptability.

This turn of events serves as a testament to his ability to anticipate and adapt to changes in business environments, a quality highly regarded in the modern entrepreneurial world. Stephen's early career not only shaped his understanding of the paint industry but also cultivated his entrepreneurial spirit. He was not discouraged by the unpredictability that the merger brought about; instead, he leveraged the situation as a catalyst for his entrepreneurial journey.

While the unpredictability of Stephen's professional life was stressful, it also fueled his ambition to create a more secure future. His decision to apply to Corporation A for duty-free concessions to manufacture paints shows a distinctive blend of foresight and determination. While still employed at the newly merged entity, he had already set his sights on creating something of his own. His application was approved on January 26th, 1972, which marked the beginning of his inspiring entrepreneurial journey.

During his time with British Paints, Stephen developed a preference for European raw materials, a direct influence of his English-based work experience. This preference later translated into the Kaleidoscope Paints Limited (KPL) approach to product quality. It was during this period that Stephen cultivated a partnership with a key chemist. When British Paints was sold to Berger Paints, the chemist returned to England, but Stephen secured his services for KPL. This strategic move allowed KPL to have their paints formulated by an experienced chemist, thus enhancing their product quality.

This chapter in Stephen's life underscores the importance of proactive thinking and decision-making in entrepreneurship. He didn't allow the uncertainty of his circumstances to paralyze him; instead, he used it as motivation to carve out a new path for himself. This mirrors the tenacity and resilience exhibited by successful entrepreneurs today, who often face setbacks and challenges before reaching their goals.

Thus, the early life of Stephen Sonny Parson provides a remarkable example of determination, resilience, and strategic thinking. It paints a picture of a man who, despite facing professional instability, chose to leverage his experiences and knowledge to create a future that was not only secure but also significantly contributed to his local community. His humble beginnings serve as an inspirational testament to the idea that great things can be achieved with passion, dedication, and an unwavering vision.

Stephen's journey showcases how he was ahead of his time, embracing qualities now celebrated in the entrepreneurial world, such as resilience, adaptability, and proactive thinking. His initial years serve as a lesson for aspiring entrepreneurs that even under difficult circumstances, one can carve out a successful path with the right mindset and an indomitable spirit.

Overview:

Chapter 1 delves into Stephen Sonny Parson's early career at British Paints (Caribbean) Limited and the transformative events that shaped his entrepreneurial spirit. Joining this company in 1955, Stephen's dedication and work ethic propelled him up the ranks, eventually becoming the Administrative Assistant to the Chairman and Managing Director. However, a merger in 1969 led to the displacement of personnel, including Stephen, prompting him to explore new opportunities. Undeterred by uncertainty, Stephen applied for duty-free concessions to manufacture paints, laying the foundation for his entrepreneurial journey. This chapter showcases Stephen's perseverance, adaptability, and strategic thinking, highlighting valuable lessons for entrepreneurs.

Key Points:

1. Stephen Sonny Parson's early career at British Paints (Caribbean) Limited marked the beginning of his lifelong relationship with the paint industry.
2. His ascent within the company demonstrated his tenacity and work ethic, eventually reaching the position of Administrative Assistant to the Chairman and Managing Director.
3. The merger of British Paints resulted in the displacement of personnel, including Stephen, prompting him to consider new avenues.
4. Stephen's resilience and adaptability enabled him to view the merger as an opportunity for entrepreneurial growth.
5. He proactively applied for duty-free concessions to manufacture paints, highlighting his foresight and determination.

6. The approval of his application on January 26th, 1972, marked the beginning of his inspiring entrepreneurial journey.

The table below displays key information related to Stephen Sonny Parson's humble beginnings:

Key Information	Details
Career Start Date	Joined British Paints (Caribbean) Limited in 1955
Professional Growth	Ascended to Administrative Assistant to the Chairman and Managing Director
Merger	British Paints (Caribbean) Limited was merged with Berger Paints
Impact of Merger	Displacement of personnel, including Stephen
Response to Change	Demonstrated resilience and adaptability
Proactive Entrepreneurial Decision	Applied for duty-free concessions to manufacture paints
Approval of Application	January 26th, 1972, marked the beginning of his entrepreneurial journey

Chapter 2

A Shift in Course – The Seeds of Resilience and Reinvention

"When you stop dreaming, you stop living." – Hasely Crawford

In 1969, an unexpected turn of events shifted the trajectory of Stephen Sonny Parson's career. British Paints, UK, to whom he had given years of dedication, decided to sell its worldwide operations to an American Chemical Company. Regrettably, the new ownership soon found the deal less than ideal, leading to the leasing of the company to Berger UK. This led to the merger of British Paints (Caribbean) Limited with Berger Trinidad.

This merger, while perhaps seen as a lucrative business deal by the parties involved, introduced a period of upheaval for the staff, especially for those occupying senior positions. It effectively dismantled the familiar structure of the company, throwing the predictability of Stephen's professional life into disarray. Yet, in this seemingly adverse circumstance, Stephen demonstrated an impressive resilience, a trait that would define his entrepreneurial journey.

The lesson in entrepreneurial adaptability that this episode provides is powerful. The modern-day business world, particularly in the wake of technological and economic changes, often presents similar challenges to those faced by Stephen. The need to swiftly adjust strategies and navigate uncertain terrains remains as relevant today as it was during Stephen's time. This ability to adapt and reinvent oneself, not just in business, but in life, underpins the narrative of many successful entrepreneurs, Stephen included.

However, this shift in his professional landscape did not signal the end for Stephen. Rather, it served as a catalytic event that paved the way for his entrepreneurial journey. In the face of uncertainty, he neither retreated nor despaired; instead, he sought opportunity. The displacement and unpredictability that he experienced underscored the importance of self-reliance, prompting him to consider a venture that would allow him to take charge of his professional destiny.

In this shift in course, Stephen demonstrated the kind of foresight and agility that separates entrepreneurs from employees. It provided him with an opportunity to hone his decision-making skills, identifying and seizing a chance to build something of his own. He looked past the apparent misfortune and saw potential, highlighting a trait common to successful entrepreneurs – the ability to view obstacles as opportunities.

The entrepreneurial spirit Stephen displayed in these circumstances was indeed ahead of his time. Today, the business landscape praises such an innovative mindset, emphasizing the necessity for entrepreneurs to think outside the box and adapt quickly to changing situations. Through his actions, Stephen offers a timeless lesson for present and future entrepreneurs: adversity often bears the seeds of innovation, and resilience is a vital trait in any entrepreneurial journey.

Despite the substantial professional setback, Stephen chose not to dwell on the disruptive change but instead to seek new horizons. This decision, to use the upheaval as a steppingstone to chart his own path, embodies the essence of entrepreneurship. It highlights the importance of resilience, adaptability, and resourcefulness, characteristics that remain central to modern entrepreneurial success stories. This chapter in Stephen's life thus stands as a testament to his foresight, reinforcing his status as a pioneering figure in entrepreneurship.

Overview:

Chapter 2 explores the unexpected turn of events that changed Stephen Sonny Parson's career trajectory. The sale of British Paints' operations led to the merger of British Paints (Caribbean) Limited with Berger Trinidad, resulting in upheaval and uncertainty for the staff. However, in the face of adversity, Stephen demonstrated remarkable resilience and adaptability. This chapter highlights the lessons of entrepreneurial adaptability and the ability to view obstacles as opportunities. It emphasizes the importance of self-reliance, foresight, and resourcefulness in navigating a changing business landscape.

Key Points:

1. The sale of British Paints' operations to an American Chemical Company led to the merger of British Paints (Caribbean) Limited with Berger Trinidad.
2. The merger disrupted the familiar structure of the company, causing upheaval and uncertainty for the staff.
3. Stephen Sonny Parson demonstrated resilience and adaptability in the face of adversity.
4. The shift in course became a catalyst for Stephen's entrepreneurial journey, prompting him to seek new horizons and take charge of his professional destiny.
5. Stephen's ability to view the disruption as an opportunity showcases the entrepreneurial mindset of thinking outside the box and seizing chances for innovation.
6. The lessons from this chapter align with the challenges faced by entrepreneurs in today's rapidly changing business landscape, emphasizing the importance of adaptability, resilience, and resourcefulness.

7. Stephen's decision to use the upheaval as a steppingstone highlights the essence of entrepreneurship and underscores the timeless value of foresight and entrepreneurial vision.

The table below depicts key information related to Stephen Sonny Parson's shift in course:

Key Information	Details
Event That Changed Career Trajectory	Sale of British Paints' operations and subsequent merger with Berger Trinidad
Disruption and Uncertainty	Upheaval caused by the merger and restructuring of the company
Stephen's Resilience and Adaptability	Demonstrated resilience and adaptability in the face of adversity
Catalyst for Entrepreneurial Journey	Shift in course prompted Stephen to seek new horizons and take charge of his professional destiny
Entrepreneurial Mindset	Viewed the disruption as an opportunity for innovation and growth
Lessons for Modern Entrepreneurs	Emphasizes the importance of adaptability, resilience, and resourcefulness in the face of change
Foresight and Vision	Stephen's ability to use the upheaval as a steppingstone showcases entrepreneurial thinking

Chapter 3

A Vision is Born

"Invention is the mother of creativity." – Winston 'Spree' Simon

As the winds of change stirred the corporate waters at Berger Trinidad, Stephen Sonny Parson developed extraordinary entrepreneur's spirit and foresight. Recognizing the precarious position of his professional future, he seized the opportunity to lay the groundwork for his independent venture. His vision was not only a reflection of his entrepreneurial acumen but also an embodiment of his inherent grit and determination.

With an unwavering belief in his abilities and potential, Stephen boldly applied to Corporation A for duty-free concessions to manufacture paints. He demonstrated a level of tenacity and audacity that would become the foundation of his entrepreneurial success. This application process was fraught with uncertainties and risks. In submitting his request, Stephen was essentially staking his career on an untested venture, demonstrating an inherent ability to shoulder risks, a key attribute of successful entrepreneurs.

His application was approved on January 26th, 1972, illuminating the path for an entrepreneurial journey that would become a source of inspiration for many. Stephen Sonny Parson's audacious decision to embark on this venture was his first significant leap of faith, a crucial step towards realizing his vision of creating a successful company. Not only does this chapter demonstrate Stephen's keen anticipation of market dynamics, but it also underscores his courage to take calculated risks in the face of uncertainty.

This decision can be compared to modern-day entrepreneurial strategies, where entrepreneurs are encouraged to seize opportunities, anticipate market shifts, and take calculated risks. Stephen Sonny Parson exemplified this modern entrepreneurial mindset decades before it became the norm. His bold decision to step away from a stable career path in pursuit of his entrepreneurial vision underscores his forward-thinking approach.

In this instance, Stephen was arguably ahead of his time. His commitment to building a future-proof venture at a time of uncertainty is reminiscent of today's entrepreneurs, who must constantly innovate and adapt to stay competitive. Moreover, Stephen's ability to transform a vision into action, a vital characteristic of successful entrepreneurs, is evident here. His decision to venture into paint manufacturing was more than just a business move; it was the birth of a vision that would significantly contribute to the paint industry's development in Trinidad and Tobago. Kaleidoscope Paints Limited became the first, 100% locally owned paint company in the late 20th century resulting from Stephen's trajectory in the local business arena.

In this chapter of his life, Stephen Sonny Parson demonstrated qualities synonymous with a visionary entrepreneur. By strategically positioning himself at the intersection of risk and opportunity, he laid the foundation for Kaleidoscope Paints Limited, showcasing his ability to leverage uncertain circumstances for his entrepreneurial advantage. His decision to embark on this venture, despite the inherent risks and challenges, is a testament to his courage, foresight, and entrepreneurial spirit.

Stephen's ability to seize opportunities in times of change is highly inspiring. As we reflect on his early ventures, it becomes clear that

Stephen was not just a man with a vision; he was a man of action. The story of Stephen Sonny Parson offers a compelling example of how resilience, foresight, and courage can transform a vision into reality. His entrepreneurial journey serves as an inspiring reminder that with the right mindset and the courage to seize opportunities, one can shape their destiny.

Overview:

Chapter 3 delves into the pivotal moment when Stephen Sonny Parson recognized the precariousness of his professional future and seized the opportunity to lay the groundwork for his independent venture. With unwavering belief in his abilities, he applied for duty-free concessions to manufacture paints. This audacious decision showcased his entrepreneurial acumen, tenacity, and ability to shoulder risks. His application was approved, marking the beginning of his entrepreneurial journey, and illuminating the path towards creating a successful company. Stephen's vision, coupled with his ability to anticipate market dynamics and take calculated risks, positions him as a forward-thinking entrepreneur who was ahead of his time.

Key Points:

1. Recognition of Precarious Position: Stephen Sonny Parson realized the need to lay the groundwork for his independent venture amid the corporate changes at Berger Trinidad.
2. Audacious Decision: He applied for duty-free concessions to manufacture paints, showcasing his entrepreneurial acumen and tenacity.
3. Ability to Shoulder Risks: By staking his career on an untested venture, Stephen demonstrated his willingness to take calculated risks, an essential attribute of successful entrepreneurs.
4. Approval of Application: Stephen's application for duty-free concessions was approved on January 26th, 1972, marking a significant milestone in his entrepreneurial journey.
5. Anticipation of Market Dynamics: Stephen's decision to venture into paint manufacturing showcased his keen

anticipation of market shifts and his ability to position himself strategically.

6. Courage and Foresight: Stephen's audacious decision to pursue his entrepreneurial vision despite the inherent risks and challenges underscored his courage and forward-thinking approach.
7. Transformation of Vision into Action: Stephen's ability to transform his vision into tangible action and establish Kaleidoscope Paints Limited reflects the characteristics of a visionary entrepreneur.
8. Lessons for Modern Entrepreneurs: Stephen's ability to seize opportunities in times of change and leverage uncertain circumstances serves as an inspiring example for entrepreneurs today.
9. Resilience, Foresight, and Courage: Stephen Sonny Parson's entrepreneurial journey highlights the importance of resilience, foresight, and courage in shaping one's destiny.

The table below showcases key information on Stephen Sonny Parson's entrepreneurial vision and the birth of Kaleidoscope Paints Limited:

Key Information	Details
Strategic Decision	Stephen's audacious decision to apply for duty-free concessions
Approval Date	January 26th, 1972
Entrepreneurial Acumen	Stephen's ability to anticipate market dynamics and position himself strategically
Risk-Taking	Demonstrated willingness to take calculated risks, a key attribute of successful entrepreneurs
Transformation of Vision into Action	Creation of Kaleidoscope Paints Limited as a tangible realization of Stephen's entrepreneurial vision
Forward-Thinking Approach	Stephen's ability to foresee market shifts and make strategic decisions ahead of his time
Lessons for Modern Entrepreneurs	Seizing opportunities in times of change, leveraging uncertain circumstances, and transforming vision into action
Courage, Foresight, and Resilience	Stephen's audacious decision, foresight, and ability to navigate challenges underscore his entrepreneurial spirit

Chapter 4

An Important Crossroad in the Business Journey

"I play to represent my people and my country. That's the highest honor." – Russell Latapy

In the early 1970s, Stephen Sonny Parson reached a significant juncture in his life. It was a moment that presented him with a stark choice, a choice that would undoubtedly determine the course of his future. On one hand, Stephen had the option to immigrate to Canada, a country renowned for providing better opportunities, a chance for a fresh start, and the prospect of a prosperous life. His children, understandably anxious about their father's frustrations at British Paints and aware of the potential rewards that lay overseas, favored this path.

On the other hand, Stephen was faced with the alternative, a riskier but potentially more rewarding opportunity. This alternative was to stay in Trinidad and forge his own path by launching a paint company, leveraging his experience and knowledge gained in the industry.

For Stephen, this decision was not simply a career choice, but a life-defining moment. It meant weighing the security and promise of a prosperous life in Canada against the unpredictable risks and rewards of entrepreneurship. After two weeks of deliberation and introspection, Stephen made his choice. He chose to remain in Trinidad, revealing his entrepreneurial spirit and deep commitment to his homeland.

The decision to start a paint company was audacious. It required significant capital, business acumen, and an unflinching spirit. Stephen, however, was not deterred. His unwavering faith in his abilities, the strength of his conviction, and his indomitable spirit propelled him forward.

The birth of his business vision saw Stephen rely on the unity and solidarity of his family members. Stephen acquired lands, which collectively measured five thousand square feet. This site, blessed with the shade of swaying coconut trees, would serve as the birthplace of Stephen's dream. It was more than just a physical location; it symbolized the collective effort of his family, their faith in Stephen's vision, and their commitment to support him on this journey.

The decision to establish his own paint company was a testament to Stephen's courage, determination, and belief in his potential. It reflected his willingness to embrace risk in pursuit of a dream and demonstrated his resilience in the face of uncertainty. Stephen's entrepreneurial journey, born from a crossroads in his life, resonates with anyone facing tough choices. It reminds us that even in the face of daunting challenges, with faith in oneself and the support of family, it is possible to follow one's dreams.

Stephen Sonny Parson's decision to build his own paint company not only changed his life but also the face of the paint industry in Trinidad. It set the foundation for Kaleidoscope Paints Limited, a company that would stand as a symbol of his ingenuity, vision, and relentless pursuit of excellence. This chapter of Stephen's life underscores the birth of a business vision, a vision that would leave a lasting impact on his family, his community, and the paint industry in Trinidad. It serves as a testament to the enduring power of dreams, determination, and the spirit of entrepreneurship.

Overview:

Chapter 4 delves into a pivotal moment in Stephen Sonny Parson's life when he faced a significant choice: to immigrate to Canada or forge his own path in Trinidad by launching a paint company. This decision was not merely a career choice but a life-defining moment that required weighing the security of a prosperous life abroad against the unpredictable risks and rewards of entrepreneurship. Stephen's unwavering faith in his abilities, deep commitment to his homeland, and entrepreneurial spirit led him to choose the latter path. With the support of his family members, Stephen acquired lands to establish his own paint company, showcasing his courage, determination, and belief in his potential. This chapter highlights the transformative power of dreams, determination, and the spirit of entrepreneurship.

Key Points:

1. Life-Defining Decision: Stephen faced the choice between immigrating to Canada for a prosperous life or launching his own paint company in Trinidad.
2. Weighing Risks and Rewards: The decision required considering the security of a comfortable life abroad versus the unpredictable risks and rewards of entrepreneurship.
3. Commitment to Homeland: Stephen's choice to remain in Trinidad reflected his deep commitment to his homeland and his desire to contribute to its development.
4. Audacious Venture: Starting a paint company required significant capital, business acumen, and an unflinching spirit, qualities Stephen possessed.
5. Unity and Support: Stephen's family members played a crucial role in his establishment of the company, symbolizing

their collective effort, faith in Stephen's vision, and commitment to support him.
6. Courage and Determination: Stephen's decision exemplified his courage, determination, and belief in his potential, demonstrating his willingness to embrace risk in pursuit of his dream.
7. Resilience in the Face of Uncertainty: The choice to launch a paint company showcased Stephen's resilience and ability to navigate uncertainty, traits essential for entrepreneurial success.
8. Transformative Impact: Stephen's decision set the foundation for Kaleidoscope Paints Limited, leaving a lasting impact on his family, community, and the paint industry in Trinidad.
9. Power of Dreams and Entrepreneurship: This chapter serves as a testament to the enduring power of dreams, determination, and the spirit of entrepreneurship in shaping one's destiny.

The table below presents important information on Stephen Sonny Parson's decision to establish his own paint company:

Key Information	Details
Decision at a Crossroad	Stephen's choice between immigrating to Canada or launching his own paint company in Trinidad
Risks and Rewards	Weighing the security of a prosperous life abroad against the unpredictable risks and rewards of entrepreneurship
Commitment to Homeland	Stephen's decision reflected his deep commitment to his homeland and desire to contribute to its development
Unity and Support	Family members' support with the establishment of the paint company
Audacity and Determination	Stephen's audacious venture showcased his courage, determination, and belief in his potential
Resilience in the Face of Uncertainty	Stephen's ability to navigate uncertainty and embrace risk in pursuit of his entrepreneurial dream
Transformative Impact	The birth of the paint company set the foundation for Kaleidoscope Paints Limited, leaving a lasting impact on the paint industry in Trinidad
Power of Dreams and Entrepreneurship	Stephen's decision exemplifies the transformative power of dreams, determination, and the entrepreneurial spirit

Chapter 5

From Coconut Lands to Paint Cans

"Hard work always pays off, whatever you do." – Dwight Yorke

In 1972, under the blistering sun and the chorus of chirping tropical birds, Stephen Sonny Parson and his family undertook an unprecedented task. The scenic coconut lands at Chanka Trace, Trinidad, laden with stubborn roots and thick brush, were to be transformed into a bustling paint factory.

Utilizing their collective strength, the family, along with friends, worked tirelessly to clear the terrain, planting the seeds for an enterprise that would soon be a symbol of local industry. Their collective endeavor was driven not by monetary gain alone, but by a shared vision for Kaleidoscope Paints Limited. They were essentially constructing not just a building but a dream, a family legacy that would become a shining example of the entrepreneurial spirit in Trinidad and Tobago.

Despite the looming financial constraints, Monica stood by Stephen's side, her presence constant, just like the support she provided. She was his rock, encouraging and helping him, even as the financial challenges threatened their dream. Their children, too, bore witness to their parents' determined work ethic, becoming an integral part of the labor force that brought Kaleidoscope Paints Limited into existence.

The task was Herculean, as the construction was initiated entirely by hand. It was a labor-intensive operation that spanned several months. Stephen, alongside his family, friends, and a few hired hands, laid the groundwork for the factory and office spaces. They dug trenches, laid the foundations, and cast the floors - a testament to their dedication and resilience. The tireless labor the Parsons poured into the construction of the factory reflected their unwavering commitment and dedication to their dream. They were not merely laying the foundation of a factory; they were laying the foundation for a family legacy and a symbol of national pride, which, with time, would blossom into one of Trinidad's most successful companies.

This scenario paints a vivid picture of Stephen's entrepreneurial spirit. It recalls modern 'bootstrapping' strategies where entrepreneurs start a business from scratch, utilizing personal savings and sweat equity, rather than relying on outside investors. Sweat equity is a term often used to describe the effort put into a project by its founders. It reflects the investment of time and labor in a project when financial resources are limited. The more the sweat equity, the more the founder's commitment to the venture. Even in the absence of abundant resources, Stephen was not deterred. Instead, he leveraged the solidarity of his community and his family's support, while sacrificing comfort and leisure, to achieve his dream.

Stephen was indeed an entrepreneur ahead of his time, leading by example and inspiring his team. His hands-on approach is comparable to the contemporary entrepreneurial practice of 'leading from the front,' where leaders actively participate in the tasks, not only commanding but also getting involved in the process.

This phase of Stephen's journey stands as a symbol of the power of community, resilience, and unity in building a business. It underlines the crucial role of human resourcefulness in entrepreneurship. It emphasizes that with clear vision, unwavering determination, and a collaborative effort, even the most challenging of tasks can be accomplished.

Despite the odds, the Parson family, led by Stephen, managed to turn a barren coconut grove into a thriving business site, foreshadowing the immense success that Kaleidoscope Paints Limited was destined to achieve. This transformation of the landscape can be likened to the metamorphosis of an entrepreneur's idea into a successful venture, highlighting Stephen's audacious ambition and ironclad resolve.

The monumental effort of creating a business enterprise from the ground up is a testament to Stephen's incredible resilience and resourcefulness. This chapter of his life serves as a beacon of inspiration for budding entrepreneurs, a reminder that success is a product of passion, patience, and persistent effort. The tale of Stephen's journey from coconut lands to a vibrant business enterprise continues to inspire and amaze, painting a picture of unwavering determination, hope, and entrepreneurial brilliance.

OVERVIEW:

Chapter 5 delves into the monumental task Stephen Sonny Parson and his family undertook in transforming the scenic coconut lands at Chanka Trace, Trinidad, into a thriving paint factory. With unwavering determination and a collaborative effort, they cleared the terrain, laid the groundwork, and cast the floors, symbolizing the birth of their entrepreneurial venture. This chapter showcases Stephen's resourcefulness, resilience, and hands-on approach, highlighting the power of community and unity in building a business.

KEY POINTS:

1. Transformation of Coconut Lands: The scenic coconut lands at Chanka Trace were transformed into a bustling paint factory through the collective effort of Stephen, his family, friends, and hired hands.
2. Herculean Task: The construction process was labor-intensive, involving clearing the terrain and manually laying the foundations for the factory and office spaces.
3. Entrepreneurial Spirit and Bootstrapping: Stephen's determination and resourcefulness are reminiscent of modern 'bootstrapping' strategies, where entrepreneurs start a business with limited resources and rely on personal savings and sweat equity.
4. Hands-On Approach: Stephen's active participation in the construction process demonstrates his hands-on approach, leading by example and inspiring his team.
5. Power of Community and Unity: The transformation of the coconut lands exemplifies the crucial role of community support, resilience, and unity in building a business.

6. Leading from the Front: Stephen's involvement in manual labor reflects the contemporary entrepreneurial practice of 'leading from the front', where leaders actively participate in tasks rather than simply delegating.
7. Entrepreneurial Metaphor: The transformation of the landscape mirrors the metamorphosis of an entrepreneur's idea into a successful venture, symbolizing Stephen's audacious ambition and unwavering resolve.
8. Resilience and Resourcefulness: Stephen's ability to overcome challenges and utilize available resources highlights his incredible resilience and resourcefulness.
9. Inspiration for Entrepreneurs: This chapter serves as an inspiration for aspiring entrepreneurs, emphasizing the importance of passion, patience, and persistent effort in building a successful enterprise.

The table below represents key information on Stephen Sonny Parson's transformation of the coconut lands into a thriving business enterprise:

Key Information	Details
Transformation of Coconut Lands	Conversion of the scenic coconut lands into a bustling paint factory
Labor-Intensive Construction	Clearing the terrain, manually laying foundations, and casting floors
Resourceful Approach	Utilization of limited resources and leveraging the support of the community
Hands-On Leadership	Stephen's active participation in the construction process, leading by example
Power of Community and Unity	Collaboration among family, friends, and hired hands in the transformation process
Entrepreneurial Metaphor	The transformation symbolizes the journey from an entrepreneur's idea to a successful business venture
Resilience and Resourcefulness	Stephen's ability to overcome challenges and make the most of available resources

Chapter 6

Strategic Investments and Financial Stewardship

"There is no magic to achievement. It's really about hard work, choices, and persistence." – Michelle-Lee Ahye

Grasping the need for financial stability, Stephen approached investors for financial assistance. The development of Stephen Sonny Parson's enterprise was marked by critical support from investors, Investor A and Investor B. He proposed a business agreement that displayed his strategic acumen - they would provide the necessary capital, and in return, earn interest when the company started generating profits. After careful consideration, Investor A and Investor B injected capital into the fledgling company.

This capital infusion was significant in fueling Stephen's dream. His entrepreneurial foresight is evident here; the strategic leveraging of personal relationships to secure funding was a calculated risk that modern entrepreneurs often adopt to bypass traditional financial hurdles. The investment by Investor A and Investor B not only affirmed the trust they had in Stephen's leadership but also acted as a testament to his ability to inspire confidence in his vision.

Additionally, this decision by Stephen Sonny Parson mirrors contemporary entrepreneurial strategies. As per the venture capital model, early investors are rewarded when the company starts making a profit. Thus, his actions showed he was ahead of his time in understanding and applying such an approach. This reflects Stephen's innovative mindset, turning his vision into a tangible business opportunity. Additionally, it is noteworthy that Stephen

Sonny Parson had no extensive qualifications in the fields of business management and finance – he had a vision and he worked tirelessly towards making this vision a reality.

Moreover, the Parson family's support emphasizes the value Stephen placed on family and close relationships. This resonates with his humble beginnings and the communal spirit that defined his early years. Even in this early stage of his venture, Stephen demonstrated that his entrepreneurial spirit was deeply rooted in a strong sense of community and familial solidarity.

While funding was an immediate hurdle, the magnitude of the challenge did not overshadow Stephen's broader vision. He understood that financial investment, although crucial, was merely a means to an end and not the end itself. This strategic comprehension of resources, financial stewardship, and long-term planning laid a solid foundation for the company's future success. He took a holistic view of entrepreneurship, which coupled with his strategic intelligence, set the stage for the incredible journey of Kaleidoscope Paints Limited.

Stephen's innovative approach to garnering financial support highlighted his entrepreneurial acumen. By turning to personal networks for funding and offering interest on returns, he not only ensured the initial capital for his dream project but also displayed an understanding of financial strategies that would become commonplace in the future world of startups and venture capital. This strategic move illustrates how Stephen Sonny Parson was not just a visionary but also a skilled entrepreneur who was truly ahead of his time. The foundation he laid and the strategies he used continue to inspire budding entrepreneurs in the present day.

Overview:

Chapter 6 delves into Stephen Sonny Parson's quest for financial stability and his strategic approach to securing investments for his enterprise. Recognizing the need for capital, Stephen turned to investor, Investor A and Investor B, proposing a business agreement where they would provide funding and earn interest once the company generated profits. Investor A and Investor B injected capital, demonstrating their trust in Stephen's leadership and his ability to inspire confidence in his vision. This chapter showcases Stephen's entrepreneurial foresight, strategic leveraging of personal relationships for funding, and his long-term planning for the company's success.

Key Points:

1. Strategic Financial Support: Stephen approached investors, Investor A and Investor B, for financial assistance, proposing an agreement where they would invest capital in exchange for interest once the company became profitable.
2. Strategic Leveraging of Personal Relationships: Stephen's approach reflects the modern entrepreneurial strategy of seeking funding from personal networks and leveraging relationships to secure investments, bypassing traditional financial hurdles.
3. Investment by Investor A and Investor B: The investment made by Investor A and Investor B affirmed their trust in Stephen's leadership and acted as a testament to his ability to inspire confidence in his vision.
4. Alignment with Contemporary Entrepreneurial Strategies: Stephen's approach aligns with the venture capital model, where early investors are rewarded when the company starts

making a profit, indicating his forward-thinking understanding of financial strategies.

5. Value on Family and Close Relationships: The support of the Parson family emphasizes Stephen's deep-rooted value for family and close relationships, echoing the communal spirit of his early years.
6. Financial Stewardship and Long-Term Planning: Stephen's strategic comprehension of resources, financial stewardship, and long-term planning laid a solid foundation for the future success of Kaleidoscope Paints Limited.
7. Holistic View of Entrepreneurship: Stephen recognized that financial investment was essential but not the sole focus, taking a holistic view of entrepreneurship and ensuring a strong foundation for the company's growth.
8. Innovative Approach and Entrepreneurial Acumen: Stephen's innovative approach to securing financial support showcased his entrepreneurial acumen and his ability to think ahead of his time.
9. Inspiration for Present-Day Entrepreneurs: Stephen's strategic moves and financial strategies continue to inspire present-day entrepreneurs, highlighting the importance of leveraging personal networks and taking a holistic approach to entrepreneurship.

The table below presents key information related to Stephen Sonny Parson's strategic investments and financial stewardship:

Key Information	Details
Strategic Financial Support	Stephen approached investors for capital investment in exchange for future interest
Leveraging Personal Relationships	Stephen's approach reflects modern entrepreneurial strategies of securing funding from personal networks
Investment by Investor A and Investor B	Investor A and Investor B injected capital, demonstrating their trust in Stephen's vision
Alignment with Contemporary Strategies	Stephen's approach aligns with the venture capital model, where early investors earn returns on profits
Value on Family and Close Relationships	The support of the Parson family reflects Stephen's commitment to family and close relationships
Financial Stewardship and Long-Term Planning	Stephen's strategic comprehension of resources and long-term planning laid a strong foundation for success
Holistic View of Entrepreneurship	Stephen recognized the importance of financial stewardship alongside other aspects of entrepreneurship
Innovative Approach and Entrepreneurial Acumen	Stephen's innovative approach showcased his entrepreneurial acumen and forward-thinking mindset

Chapter 7

Opposition and Perseverance

"You don't drown by falling in the water; you drown by staying there." – Edwin Roberts

Stephen Sonny Parson's entrepreneurial journey was not a path free of resistance; in fact, it was marked by significant opposition. When word reached competitors about Stephen's venture, they sought to undermine his progress. This was a particularly challenging and discouraging period for Stephen, leaving him fraught with frustration and worry that his vision might be jeopardized.

Nevertheless, Stephen's astute entrepreneurial instinct compelled him to persist. He navigated through the turbulence with strength and a sharp focus on his mission. He intuitively knew that success lay not just in the ability to persevere, but also in creating a network of allies who would support his cause. Thus, he drew on his impressive networking skills, leveraging relationships he had nurtured over the years.

In April 1972, his resilience paid off. After dogged negotiations, Stephen secured a critical loan of one hundred thousand dollars ($100,000) from Corporation B. This was a testament to his persuasive communication skills and the credibility he had built as a competent professional in the paint industry. In present-day entrepreneurship, these traits are recognized as invaluable for winning investor confidence.

This chapter in Stephen's life provides an insightful entrepreneurial lesson. Modern entrepreneurs face numerous challenges in the form of competition, regulatory hurdles, and financial constraints. Stephen's example teaches them the value of perseverance, networking, and the importance of developing a credible personal brand. His strategies, although implemented in the early 1970s, are timeless, universally applicable, and serve as an inspiration for today's entrepreneurs.

However, his brilliance goes beyond these aspects. Stephen's ability to turn adversities into opportunities shows his forward-thinking attitude, a quality that separates great entrepreneurs from merely good ones. Today, in a world filled with startups, his story stands as a testament to the importance of tenacity and creativity in overcoming challenges, demonstrating that he was truly ahead of his time.

His narrative also illuminates the value of adaptability, another quality crucial in modern entrepreneurship. When faced with adversity, instead of succumbing, Stephen adapted and shifted his strategy to safeguard his vision. This adaptability showcases a trait that is imperative in today's rapidly changing business environment, where entrepreneurs must constantly adapt their strategies to keep up with market dynamics and customer needs.

Ultimately, Stephen Sonny Parson was not just a paint manufacturer; he was a trailblazing entrepreneur. His entrepreneurial strategies, combined with his perseverance and resilience, are invaluable lessons for anyone aspiring to create a business or innovate within an existing one. His story, therefore, continues to inspire and motivate, proving that with steadfast determination and the right strategies, one can overcome challenges and achieve remarkable success.

Overview:

Chapter 7 of Stephen Sonny Parson's biography delves into the challenges and opposition he faced during his entrepreneurial journey. Competitors sought to undermine his progress, causing frustration and concern for the future of his venture. However, Stephen's perseverance and strategic thinking propelled him forward. He leveraged his networking skills and nurtured relationships to build a supportive network. Through tenacity and effective communication, he secured a crucial loan for one hundred thousand dollars ($100,000) loan from Corporation B in April 1972.

Key Points:

1. Overcoming opposition: Stephen encountered resistance from competitors who aimed to undermine his progress, but his determination and focus allowed him to navigate through the turbulent times.
2. Networking and relationship-building: Stephen drew on his strong network of allies and nurtured relationships to gain support for his venture.
3. Persuasive communication skills: Stephen's credibility in the paint industry and his ability to effectively communicate his vision played a crucial role in securing a loan for one hundred thousand dollars ($100,000) from Corporation B.
4. Perseverance and adaptability: Stephen's story illustrates the importance of perseverance in the face of challenges and the need for adaptability to adjust strategies and overcome obstacles.
5. Timeless entrepreneurial lessons: The strategies and qualities demonstrated by Stephen, such as perseverance, networking, and adaptability, serve as valuable lessons for present-day entrepreneurs facing similar challenges.

CHAPTER 8

KEY CHARACTERISTICS OF A SKILLED ENTREPRENEUR

"We are not just a people with a rich heritage, we are the heritage."
– Hollis "Chalkdust" Liverpool

In the latter half of 1972, Stephen Sonny Parson walked into Corporation C, not merely as an aspiring businessman, but as an expert in his field. He sought an audience with the corporation's manager, to secure additional financial backing for his fledgling enterprise, presenting himself as a knowledgeable entrepreneur with a well-founded business plan.

His extensive industry experience and in-depth understanding of paint manufacturing, garnered over many years, resonated with the manager. Parson's confident demeanor, coupled with a deep passion for his craft, painted a clear picture of an ambitious man ready to transform the paint industry in Trinidad. The careful combination of technical knowledge and entrepreneurial vision helped Parson secure the approval of an overdraft facility for one hundred thousand dollars ($100,000), further solidifying his position as an emerging player in the business arena.

Securing this significant financial aid was not without its risks. Parson had to establish personal guarantees and life insurance policies assigned to the corporation. It was a bold move, reflective of his unwavering belief in the potential of his business idea and its ability to succeed. This bold move was exemplified in the fact that Stephen had to take care of a household of fourteen members and was the sole breadwinner. This strategy echoes modern-day entrepreneurial methods, where founders often must personally guarantee loans or stake their personal assets to acquire funding for their startups. Parson's commitment to his vision showcases a daring entrepreneurial strategy that is as relevant today as it was in his time.

Additionally, his ability to persuade a large corporation, personified by the manager, to back his enterprise echoes the necessity for entrepreneurs to foster robust relationships and cultivate networks. This pivotal act of securing funding highlighted Parson's aptitude for leveraging connections, a practice widely regarded as an essential entrepreneurial skill in today's corporate world. His ability to present his case convincingly to the manager, to build rapport, and to instill confidence in his business venture was a testament to his persuasive communication skills and strategic networking.

Stephen Sonny Parson's approach, particularly his early embodiment of lean start-up principles, was remarkably ahead of his time. He invested not just in the creation of a product, but also in the build-up of a brand that would eventually resonate with the local populace. Stephen was a trailblazer who could marry technical expertise with an astute business acumen. His decision to bank on effective communication to further his business objectives underscores the power of networking, principles that modern entrepreneurs continue to swear by.

Parson's actions were a remarkable testament to his belief in himself and his dream. It shows his willingness to take calculated risks, grounded in in-depth industry knowledge and a robust, inspiring vision, which is a trait shared by many successful entrepreneurs. His strategic thinking, forward-planning, determination, deep-rooted belief in his vision and relationship-building skills laid the foundation for his entrepreneurial journey, a journey that was not merely about business, but about inspiring others and fostering a legacy.

Despite the mounting challenges, Stephen remained resilient, drawing on the strength and support of his family to transform his entrepreneurial dream into a tangible, thriving reality. Such fortitude, perseverance, and familial teamwork were emblematic of Stephen's unique entrepreneurial spirit, setting a high benchmark for modern entrepreneurs. His entrepreneurial strategies, work ethics, and family involvement are a testament to how a strong and shared vision can overcome the most daunting challenges. He was indeed a visionary ahead of his time, an inspiration not only to his family and community but to every budding entrepreneur in the world.

This chapter of Stephen Sonny Parson's life brings to light his adept entrepreneurship and his audacious and determined spirit. It showcases his ability to convince and inspire others with his vision and dedication, illustrating the brilliance of his entrepreneurial strategies. It also serves as a testament to the tireless dedication, resilience, and family camaraderie that went into building a successful business from scratch, setting the stage for the triumphant rise of Kaleidoscope Paints Limited. Parson stands out as an exemplar, not just for his time but for aspiring entrepreneurs today, embodying the spirit of innovation, resilience, and relentless pursuit of a dream.

Overview:

Chapter 8 explores a crucial turning point in Stephen Sonny Parson's entrepreneurial journey. Armed with his industry expertise and a well-founded business plan, Stephen approached Corporation C for additional financial backing. His confident demeanor, technical knowledge, and passionate vision resonated with the corporation's manager leading to the approval of an overdraft facility of one hundred thousand dollars ($100,000)..

Key Points:

1. Technical expertise and entrepreneurial vision: Parson's deep understanding of paint manufacturing, coupled with his ambitious entrepreneurial vision, played a significant role in securing financial backing from Corporation C.
2. Personal guarantees and calculated risks: Parson's commitment to his business was evident in his willingness to provide personal guarantees and life insurance policies as collateral for the financial aid, reflecting the common practice of founders staking personal assets for funding in modern-day entrepreneurship.
3. Leveraging connections and persuasive communication: Parson's ability to persuade the corporation's manager highlights the importance of cultivating networks and building strong relationships as an essential entrepreneurial skill.
4. Strategic thinking and forward-planning: Parson's approach demonstrated his strategic thinking and ability to present a well-founded business plan, showcasing the significance of foresight and planning in entrepreneurial success.

Chapter 9

Building the Board

"Your past is your strength." – Jit Samaroo

A deep understanding of the importance of connections and interpersonal relationships led Stephen Sonny Parson to approach prominent figures such as Contact A, Contact B, Director A, and Director B, inviting them to invest and join his ambitious endeavor. His pitch was not merely an invitation to invest money, but to be a part of a remarkable journey, a journey to create a prestigious organization that would revolutionize the paint industry in Trinidad.

To Stephen, each of these individuals represented more than just potential capital; they were seasoned entrepreneurs, influencers in their respective fields, and the embodiment of prestige and success that he wanted for his enterprise. Assembling this distinguished team was a strategic move akin to the present-day trend of attracting influential board members or advisors to increase a startup's reputation and connections. This strategy, which is prevalent in the modern entrepreneurial landscape, is yet another testament to Stephen's forward-thinking mindset.

While Contacts A and B declined to join his ambitious venture, Directors A and B, enthralled by Stephen's vision, accepted the roles of Chairman and Director, respectively. They not only contributed capital but also brought their expertise, influence, and networks to the table. This infusion of monetary capital, expertise and intellect by these persons was a significant turning point in the journey of Kaleidoscope Paints Limited.

Despite being in the nascent stages of his entrepreneurial journey, Stephen demonstrated an entrepreneurial instinct reminiscent of successful modern-day startups. He understood that an organization's success does not merely hinge on financial capital; instead, it is the amalgamation of financial, intellectual, and social capital. This understanding that drove him to approach individuals like Directors A and B was an entrepreneurial move well ahead of his time, highlighting his innate business acumen.

The addition of Directors A and B to the company's leadership portfolio expanded the sphere of influence of Kaleidoscope Paints Limited. Their capital contributions provided the needed financial stability, allowing Stephen to focus more on operational and strategic facets of the business. This step is akin to modern-day fundraising rounds where entrepreneurs look for 'smart money'— investments from those who can also contribute their expertise and network for the company's benefit.

Stephen had a knack for spotting talent, as is evident from the long-serving members that joined him from other companies. His ability to build a committed team laid the foundation for KPL's longevity, a testament to his vision and entrepreneurial acumen. One key figure who stood beside Parson in the early days was a brilliant tax accountant. He provided invaluable financial advice and helped navigate legal challenges. Today, the importance of strategic advisors and mentors in entrepreneurship is well-recognized.

The alignment of his vision with influential personalities such as Directors A and B speaks volumes about Stephen's charisma and ability to inspire confidence in others about his plans. This skill, coupled with his strategic and financial acumen, underscored his extraordinary entrepreneurial capabilities.

In his pursuit of prestige for his company, Stephen Sonny Parson was laying the foundations of an organization that would become a beacon of success and innovation in the Trinidad paint industry. His keen understanding of the power of strategic partnerships, his unwavering determination to create a prestigious organization, and his ability to inspire confidence in his vision, marked the initial strides of a journey that would eventually make Kaleidoscope Paints Limited a household name in Trinidad.

Overview:

Chapter 9 delves into Stephen Sonny Parson's strategic approach to building his network of influential individuals who would contribute not only financially but also intellectually to the success of Kaleidoscope Paints Limited. By approaching figures like Contacts A and B as well as Directors A and B, Stephen aimed to assemble a distinguished team that would revolutionize the paint industry in Trinidad.

Key Points:

1. Leveraging influential connections: Stephen recognized the value of influential individuals in his network and approached them to join his venture, mirroring the modern entrepreneurial trend of attracting influential board members or advisors to enhance a startup's reputation and connections.
2. Seeking intellectual and social capital: Stephen understood that success extended beyond financial capital, and thus, sought individuals who could contribute their expertise, influence, and networks to the company.
3. Expansion of influence: The addition of Directors A and B to the company's leadership expanded the sphere of influence of KPL, providing financial stability and allowing Stephen to focus on operational and strategic aspects of the business.
4. Strategic partnerships as a foundation: Stephen's ability to align his vision with influential personalities and inspire confidence underscored his entrepreneurial capabilities and set the stage for the future success of KPL.
5. Pursuit of prestige: Stephen's determination to create a prestigious organization drove his efforts in building a team of influential individuals.

Chapter 10

A Tale of Family and Faith

"We are all one people." – Dr. Eric Williams

Despite the numerous responsibilities and challenges that accompanied Stephen Sonny Parson's entrepreneurial journey, he was, above all else, a devoted family man. Guiding a family constituting fourteen members, while also leading a company through its foundational stages, Stephen showed his innate ability to nurture a harmonious environment.

Discipline and cooperation were two core values that Stephen instilled in his children from an early age. As the day's first light spilled into their family home, the children would find their father already awake and beginning his day's work. This routine of early rising was not just a practical necessity for Stephen; it was a philosophy, an expression of his belief in making the most of each day. Along with this, he emphasized the importance of sharing household chores, teaching his children that every task, however mundane, carried its own dignity and value.

Despite the intense demands of his business, Stephen consistently prioritized his family. He made it a point to create memorable experiences for them, especially birthdays, Mother's Day, Father's Day as well as New Year's Eve, frequently treating them to Chinese dinners, an unconventional choice that reflected his adventurous spirit. His spirit was also remembered through his passion towards Indian and vintage music, having his own personal, extensive, music collection, as well as his cooking, including dishes such as "curried goat". Stephen's dedication to his family extended beyond shared meals. He orchestrated family vacations to Mayaro, Wallerfield and even outside of Trinidad, demonstrating a belief in the restorative power of leisure and togetherness. Additionally, he fostered a strong connection with the extended family, arranging regular visits that upheld the familial bond and ensured that his children understood the importance of family unity.

Parallel to his devotion to family, there was a deep-rooted faith. Stephen was a pillar of the community Presbyterian Church, whose tenets echoed in his life's philosophy. This was not a passive faith but an active engagement with his religious community, through which he became friends with a local, prominent reverend. He contributed significantly to the church's development, both through significant financial support and active participation in its community programs, including his presidency and participation in the Men's Group in 1968.

His presence and generosity can still be felt in the community Presbyterian Church today, where the beautiful church organ he contributed to, the Allen Digital Computer Organ System MDS-5, as well as his other infrastructural donations, are appreciated by its congregation. Stephen's faith was not merely an aspect of his personal life; it influenced his professional decisions and the ethos of Kaleidoscope Paints Limited, imbuing the company's culture with principles of honesty, integrity, and respect.

Stephen's commitment to his faith and family mirrored the same dedication he applied to his professional life. This seamless blend of personal values with professional ambitions was a cornerstone of his character, reflecting the interweaving of different aspects of his life into a unified whole. His deep faith provided a moral compass, guiding his actions and decisions both at home and at work.

Reflecting on this chapter of Stephen Sonny Parson's life, we see a man who managed to strike a delicate balance between professional ambition and personal fulfillment. He cultivated a thriving business while also fostering a supportive, loving family environment and actively participating in his faith community. His life illustrates that success is not measured merely by professional accomplishments but also by the strength of one's relationships and the impact one has on their community.

Stephen's legacy is not confined to the thriving business of Kaleidoscope Paints Limited. It is also embedded in the values and traditions he passed on to his children, the strength of the family bonds he nurtured, and the significant contributions he made to his church community. His life serves as an enduring inspiration, reminding us that true fulfillment comes from leading a balanced life, underpinned by steadfast values, strong relationships, and a dedication to serving one's community.

OVERVIEW:

Chapter 10 delves into Stephen Sonny Parson's unwavering commitment to his family and faith throughout his entrepreneurial journey. Despite the demands of building and leading a company, Stephen prioritized his family, instilling core values of discipline and cooperation in his children. He created memorable experiences and nurtured strong family bonds through shared meals, vacations, and regular visits with the extended family. Additionally, Stephen's deep-rooted faith in the Presbyterian Church of Trinidad and Tobago influenced his personal and professional life. His active engagement with the church community and financial support reflected his commitment to honesty, integrity, and respect.

KEY POINTS:

1. Core values: Stephen instilled discipline and cooperation in his children, teaching them the dignity and value of every task.
2. Creating memorable experiences: Stephen prioritized creating memorable experiences for his family through shared meals and orchestrated vacations, fostering strong family bonds.
3. Extended family unity: Stephen emphasized the importance of maintaining strong connections with the extended family, arranging regular visits to uphold familial bonds.
4. Deep-rooted faith: Stephen's faith in the Presbyterian Church of Trinidad and Tobago influenced his personal and professional decisions, guiding his actions with principles of honesty, integrity, and respect.
5. Balancing personal and professional life: Stephen's ability to strike a balance between professional ambition and personal fulfillment serves as an inspiration.

Chapter 11

The Birth of Kaleidoscope Paints Limited

"Each stroke of the brush is a step towards creating history."
– Boscoe Holder

Stephen Sonny Parson's life was anything but ordinary. In the early 1970s, Trinidad and Tobago was a nation grappling with its recent independence. Having shed its colonial status in 1962 and on its way to becoming a Republic, the nation was in the throes of significant economic changes. The shift from a predominantly sugar cane cultivation-based economy to diversified sectors opened the door for foreign companies to flood the market, providing formidable competition to local businesses.

It was during these years of economic flux that Stephen Sonny Parson embarked on a daring venture. Previously known as Sonny Parsan, he made the strategic decision to change his name, in what was essentially an act of adaptability. The name "Parson", while maintaining a connection to his roots, had a more universal resonance, and was a strategic maneuver aimed at carving out an identity in the global market.

In a way, Stephen's name change represented the spirit of an entire era, where traditional identities were being renegotiated and reinvented in the face of new global realities. This bold move wasn't merely cosmetic; it was a statement of intent, signaling his readiness to operate on the global stage and compete with foreign brands on equal terms.

In the context of his business, Stephen's name change served as a means of elevating his nascent company amidst a competitive market saturated with foreign-owned entities. As the founder of Kaleidoscope Paints Limited, his change of name conveyed an understanding of the importance of adaptability, an entrepreneurial strategy that continues to be paramount in today's business world.

In retrospect, Stephen Sonny Parson's decision to alter his name was an act of strategic positioning within an evolving market. In the face of steep competition and the challenges inherent to a newly independent nation seeking its economic footing, he remained steadfast in his vision. His story serves as a testament to the entrepreneurial spirit, highlighting his willingness to adapt and innovate in the pursuit of success. His strategies, conceived in a time of drastic change, are testament to a brilliant mind that was not only in step with his era but arguably, far ahead of his time. Stephen Sonny Parson's legacy continues to inspire, reminding us that adaptability and a keen sense of market dynamics remain key to thriving in any economic climate.

Having started from the humble beginnings of clearing coconut lands, the year 1973 marked a significant milestone for him and his family. They inaugurated a venture that was more than just a business—it was a collective passion. The family, along with a small group of diligent workers, took on the task of establishing the factory that became the cradle of Kaleidoscope Paints Limited. They poured their hearts and souls into this venture, from labelling paint tins to promoting products, and even serving as models for advertising campaigns.

This hands-on involvement in every aspect of the business embodied an entrepreneurial principle that is lauded today—embracing multiple roles within a start-up. Parson seemed to be ahead of his time, acting out a concept that is now recognized as an integral part of start-up culture. This dedication is reminiscent of modern entrepreneurs who are not just business heads but also the face of their brand, working tirelessly across functions, mirroring Parson's own strategy.

The name, Kaleidoscope Paints Limited, a shift from the original "Trinidad Paints Limited" was made official on October 9th, 1973. This rebranding signified the vibrant and transformative nature of the company, symbolizing the myriad of colors they offered and the diverse clientele they served. It's striking to note how Parson's foresight in branding anticipated the significance of impactful branding in today's globalized world. The colorful and dynamic identity of Kaleidoscope Paints Limited not only gave the company a unique recognition but also enhanced its overall value, reminiscent of how successful companies today invest heavily in crafting meaningful and unique brand identities.

Parson's entrepreneurial journey was not a solo endeavor. He strongly believed in the power of collective effort; a strategy employed by many modern businesses that underscores the importance of teamwork. This was reflected in his efforts to make everyone around him an integral part of the company's journey. Involving his family in the core business operations not only gave them a sense of ownership and commitment but also brought a personal touch to the business. This helped build a strong connection with customers, which further strengthened the brand – being known as a family brand; a household staple of quality.

His commitment to business and his intuitive approach to overcoming challenges laid the groundwork for Kaleidoscope Paints Limited. This dedication can be likened to the passion exhibited by successful entrepreneurs today who, when confronted with challenges, persevere until they achieve their goals. Parson was not deterred by the roadblocks he encountered but instead found ways to overcome them, embodying the entrepreneurial spirit that continues to inspire future generations of business leaders.

In retrospect, Stephen Sonny Parson was not just building a business; he was building a legacy. A legacy that was born out of a vision, a vision that was brought to life by a man and his family who dared to dream and dared to achieve. His remarkable journey from a simple paint company employee to the founder of one of Trinidad's most successful paint companies is a testament to his unwavering determination, his innovative spirit, and his extraordinary leadership. It's a story that continues to inspire and motivate, painting a vivid picture of a man who was not only ahead of his time but who also left a lasting mark on the canvas of entrepreneurial history.

Overview:

Chapter 11 narrates the transformative moment when Stephen Sonny Parson and his family officially established Kaleidoscope Paints Limited in 1973. Their hands-on involvement in all aspects of the business exemplified the entrepreneurial principle of embracing multiple roles within a start-up. Parson's foresight in rebranding the company as Kaleidoscope Paints Limited showcased his understanding of the importance of impactful branding in today's globalized world.

Key Points:

1. Embracing multiple roles: Parson's hands-on involvement in all aspects of the business exemplified the entrepreneurial principle of embracing multiple roles within a start-up, a concept recognized as integral in today's start-up culture.
2. Strategic rebranding: The rebranding of the company as Kaleidoscope Paints Limited showcased Parson's foresight in understanding the significance of impactful branding, setting the company apart and enhancing its recall value.
3. Power of collective effort: Parson involved his family in the core business operations, creating a sense of ownership and commitment while building a strong connection with customers, mirroring the importance of teamwork and personal touch in modern businesses.
4. Unwavering determination: Parson's dedication and intuitive approach to overcoming challenges laid the groundwork for the birth of Kaleidoscope Paints Limited.
5. Building a legacy: Parson's journey from a paint company employee to the founder of a successful company exemplifies his unwavering determination, innovative spirit, and extraordinary leadership.

Chapter 12

The Challenges of Growth

"Our strength lies in our diversity." – Ralph Maraj

The nascent stages of Kaleidoscope Paints Limited witnessed rapid growth, a testament to Stephen Sonny Parson's entrepreneurial spirit and hard work. However, this phase was not without its challenges, particularly the strain on familial relationships due to financial entanglements. Investor B began expressing discomfort with the lack of tangible evidence for his considerable financial contributions to the business. Rather than allowing this concern to fester and potentially unravel the business, Stephen navigated this hurdle with commendable grace and business acumen.

Stephen chose to demonstrate his integrity and commitment to transparency in business dealings by issuing Share Certificates to Investor A and Investor B. This action served as a tangible reassurance to his investors of their investment's acknowledgment and a physical testament to their invaluable contribution to the burgeoning enterprise. Stephen's decision to address Investor B's concerns in this manner exemplified his astute understanding of the need for clear and transparent financial dealings and highlighted his commitment to maintaining a trusting and harmonious business environment.

Stephen's action demonstrates a quality that modern-day entrepreneurs often struggle to embody: the understanding that the growth of a business can create internal pressures and tensions, and the ability to swiftly address these issues to prevent them from hindering progress. His approach to resolving potential conflicts foreshadowed the emerging concept of "conscious capitalism", which emphasizes a holistic approach to business, considering the needs and concerns of all stakeholders.

As Kaleidoscope Paints Limited continued to expand, Stephen's innovative and proactive strategies not only met the challenges of growth but also fostered a climate of trust and integrity. These attributes are integral to the sustainability and success of any business, transcending time, and changes in the business landscape. Therefore, Stephen Sonny Parson was truly ahead of his time, embodying entrepreneurial principles that continue to be heralded as revolutionary in the contemporary business world.

This period in Stephen's journey brings to light the complexities of managing growth and the potential difficulties that can arise from mixing business with personal relationships. It showcases Stephen's wisdom in addressing potential conflicts head-on and his commitment to upholding transparency, making him a remarkably inspiring figure.

His decisive actions during this challenging period further solidify his standing as an entrepreneur who was not only capable of creating and expanding a business but also of maintaining and nurturing relationships within it. Through this, he reminds us that successful entrepreneurship is not just about capital and ideas but also about integrity, transparency, and trust.

Overview:

Chapter 12 explores the challenges that accompanied the rapid growth of Kaleidoscope Paints Limited and how Stephen Sonny Parson navigated these hurdles with grace and business acumen. Stephen addressed shareholder concerns by issuing Share Certificates, demonstrating integrity and transparency in business dealings. This action showcased Stephen's commitment to maintaining a trusting and harmonious business environment. His approach exemplified the emerging concept of "conscious capitalism" and highlighted the importance of addressing internal pressures and tensions to sustain business growth.

Key Points:

1. Strain on shareholder relationships: Rapid growth created strains with shareholders due to financial entanglements, highlighting the complexities of mixing business with shareholder personal relationships.
2. Commitment to transparency: Stephen's issuance of Share Certificates to address shareholder concerns demonstrated his commitment to transparency in financial dealings and ensuring trust.
3. Conscious capitalism: Stephen's approach foreshadowed the emerging concept of conscious capitalism, emphasizing a holistic approach to business that considers the needs and concerns of all stakeholders.
4. Managing growth challenges: Stephen's innovative and proactive strategies met the challenges of growth, fostering trust and integrity within the company.
5. Wisdom and integrity: Stephen's decisive actions during this challenging period solidify his standing as an entrepreneur.

Chapter 13

A Symphony of Family Unity and Entrepreneurship

"In the end, it's not the years in your life that count. It's the life in your years." – George Bailey

The story of Stephen Sonny Parson's success cannot be told without recounting the significant role his family played in it. In the whirlwind of creating a burgeoning business, his family was not only his rock of support but also an integral part of the workforce that drove Kaleidoscope Paints Limited forward.

Monica, Stephen's wife, proved to be a bedrock of support throughout the journey. Her contributions went far beyond the traditional roles of a wife. Amid the tumultuous times of building a business from scratch, she became the company's first typist, working diligently, for twelve (12) hours and more each day for several years, to ensure the smooth flow of administrative work. This was a testimony to her adaptability, her willingness to learn, and her commitment to the family's shared dream.

Monica's contribution extended beyond her work on the typewriter. She embodied the spirit of a homegrown enterprise, often preparing meals for the staff at company celebrations and parties. Monica, together with Stephen's two children, became an integral part of the company's promotional efforts. They generously lent their images to newspaper advertisements for KPL's products, adding a personal touch to the promotions. These acts were not only an expression of familial warmth but also smart and practical approaches to minimize costs during the company's infancy.

Moreover, Monica's brothers made invaluable contributions to the budding company. They authored and produced the company's first jingle, providing an early boost to Kaleidoscope Paints' marketing efforts. This use of in-house resources for marketing was not only cost-effective but also allowed for a personalized touch in the company's brand identity, which was unique at the time and still stands out in the digital marketing era today.

The involvement of Stephen's entire family in the business blurred the lines between work and home, creating a unique synergy of unity and entrepreneurial spirit. Stephen and his family's endeavor exemplifies the saying, "the family that works together, stays together". It demonstrated that nurturing a shared dream could forge an unbreakable bond, transcending the traditional family-business relationship.

Stephen Sonny Parson's journey serves as a masterclass in building a business from the ground up, illustrating that the incorporation of family and community in a business setting can be a successful strategy. It defies the oft-repeated entrepreneurial advice of keeping business and personal life separate. Stephen utilized available resources effectively, tapping into the talents and skills of his family members to reduce costs, a strategy quite like bootstrapping in modern-day entrepreneurial parlance.

Stephen's approach was years ahead of its time. It predates the present trend of "startup culture", where everyone involved in a business, irrespective of their roles, is seen as contributing to its success. This family-oriented approach not only ensured the efficient utilization of resources but also created a sense of ownership and commitment within each member, crucial factors that contributed to the resilience of Kaleidoscope Paints Limited in its initial years.

In contrast to the dominant models of corporate hierarchy, Stephen's approach was more akin to a cooperative model, encouraging participation from all members of the family. This involvement of family members in different roles can be compared to the cross-functional teams in today's startup culture, enhancing adaptability and ensuring that each task was handled by someone who truly cared about the company's success.

The spirit of unity, adaptability, and the relentless pursuit of a shared dream that permeated the Parson family's work style was instrumental in building the foundation of Kaleidoscope Paints Limited. They defied traditional business norms, presenting a remarkable example of entrepreneurial innovation and perseverance. This approach continues to inspire modern entrepreneurs, proving that strong familial bonds and shared dreams can indeed be a successful recipe for an entrepreneurial journey.

Overview:

Chapter 13 explores the integral role of Stephen Sonny Parson's family in the success of Kaleidoscope Paints Limited. Monica, Stephen's wife, played a significant supportive role, taking on administrative tasks and providing meals for the staff. The involvement of Monica's brothers in marketing efforts added a personal touch to the company's brand identity. This chapter showcases the synergy between family unity and entrepreneurship, challenging the notion of separating personal and professional life. Stephen's approach of incorporating family members into the business exemplifies resourcefulness and the cooperative model.

Key Points:

1. Monica's contributions: Monica went beyond traditional roles, becoming the company's typist and providing meals for the staff, demonstrating adaptability, and cost-effectiveness.
2. In-house marketing: Monica's brothers authored and produced the company's first jingle, showcasing the use of in-house resources for personalized and cost-effective marketing.
3. Family unity and entrepreneurship: The involvement of Stephen's entire family created a unique synergy, defying the separation of personal and professional life, and fostering a shared dream.
4. Resource utilization: Stephen tapped into the talents and skills of his family members, reducing costs and exhibiting a bootstrap-like approach.
5. Cooperative model: Stephen's approach mirrored a cooperative model, involving family members in different roles, similar to modern-day cross-functional teams in startups, enhancing adaptability and commitment.

CHAPTER 14

THE RESILIENT PATH TO SUCCESS

"It always seems impossible until it's done." – Nelson Mandela

Stephen Sonny Parson's story is one of unwavering perseverance, embodied by his undying dedication to his craft. Working eighteen hours a day, seven days a week, he demonstrated a resolve seldom found in ordinary individuals. His tenacity was further underscored when, even after a double bypass operation in 1982, he resumed work, defying his physician's counsel. It was as if his love for the company and the dream it represented was a life force that nothing, not even health issues, could diminish.

His multifaceted roles within the company mirrored his versatility and commitment. Not only did Parson serve as the Managing Director, but he also undertook multiple roles as the Technical Manager, Sales and Marketing Manager, Financial Controller, Advertising Manager, and Customs Manager. This plethora of responsibilities, far from deterring him, instead fueled his passion and his resolution to make Kaleidoscope Paints Limited a resounding success.

From an entrepreneurial perspective, his work ethic was not merely a testament to his grit but also an exemplar of his ability to adapt to the requirements of the burgeoning business. By taking on multiple roles, Parson demonstrated a level of operational flexibility that allowed the company to maximize its resources, a principle that many modern entrepreneurs would find valuable in the initial stages of a start-up. This was not just an entrepreneurial strategy; it was a survival technique that secured the company's foothold in the competitive paint industry.

What was remarkable about Parson's journey was not just his resilience and his ability to wear many hats but also his innovative spirit. He was continually seeking ways to improve and innovate, much ahead of his time. His relentless pursuit of innovation, coupled with his deep knowledge of the industry, helped to differentiate Kaleidoscope Paints from its competitors.

The entrepreneur's strategy of diversifying roles could be likened to modern business practices, like lean startup methodology, where an entrepreneur takes on various roles in the initial stages of a business to conserve resources. His strategies resonate with the present day, proving him to be a visionary who was ahead of his time.

Stephen Sonny Parson's indomitable spirit, relentless dedication, and innovative mindset were key to his success and were foundational in creating the legacy of Kaleidoscope Paints Limited. These elements combined to form a powerful tapestry, serving as a testament to the inspirational life of this remarkable entrepreneur. His story continues to resonate, teaching entrepreneurs the importance of perseverance, dedication, and innovation in carving a successful business journey. His life serves as a guiding light, illuminating the path for many future entrepreneurs.

Overview:

Chapter 14 delves into Stephen Sonny Parson's unwavering perseverance and dedication to his craft. Despite health challenges, including a double bypass operation, he resumed work, driven by his love for Kaleidoscope Paints Limited. Parson's multifaceted roles within the company showcased his versatility and commitment, taking on responsibilities across various functions. His ability to adapt and wear many hats exemplified operational flexibility, a survival technique that secured the company's foothold in the competitive paints industry. Parson's relentless pursuit of innovation and his innovative mindset helped differentiate Kaleidoscope Paints from competitors, solidifying his status as a visionary entrepreneur ahead of his time.

Key Points:

1. Unwavering perseverance: Parson's dedication to his craft was unwavering, as seen by his commitment to working long hours and resuming work after health challenges.
2. Multifaceted roles: Parson served in multiple capacities within the company, showcasing his versatility and commitment to making Kaleidoscope Paints a success.
3. Operational flexibility: Parson's ability to adapt and take on multiple roles maximized resources and ensured the company's foothold in the competitive paints industry.
4. Relentless pursuit of innovation: Parson's innovative spirit and constant search for improvement set Kaleidoscope Paints apart from competitors.
5. Resonance with modern practices: Parson's strategy of diversifying roles aligns with lean startup methodology, showcasing his visionary approach.

Chapter 15

A Visionary Leader in the Twentieth Century

"Every note I play is a part of my story." – Ella Andall

The entrepreneurial journey of Stephen Sonny Parson symbolizes a vivid palette of perseverance, innovation, and leadership. With Kaleidoscope Paints Limited, he created not just an enterprise, but a profound legacy that continues to inspire generations. Parson's story represents a rich tapestry woven with threads of humility, resilience, and an unyielding vision.

Born in an era devoid of the technological conveniences we take for granted today, Parson foresaw a future where local paint production could redefine Trinidad's market. His entrepreneurial spirit was not driven by mere ambition for wealth; instead, he sought to create an impactful change. The inception and subsequent success of Kaleidoscope Paints Limited serves as an embodiment of his entrepreneurial acumen and unwavering commitment.

Parson's strategic approach to business sets a benchmark for modern-day entrepreneurship. He effectively utilized available resources, successfully transforming barren lands into a thriving factory. By identifying and leveraging his connections, Parson ensured financial stability for his venture in its infancy. His determination to preserve integrity and transparency in business, aligns with the ethos of contemporary entrepreneurial practice.

Parson's leadership style was characterized by a strong belief in human potential, aptly demonstrated through the integral roles his family played in the growth of the company. This faith in human resources is echoed in today's successful businesses that prioritize a people-centric approach, recognizing the vital role employees play in driving growth.

Through strategic alliances with influential professionals of his time, Parson built credibility for his venture. His collaborative approach mirrors the modern concept of strategic partnerships, a crucial aspect of today's dynamic entrepreneurial landscape.

Moreover, Parson was a forward-thinker who understood the value of branding. His decision to change the name of his company to Kaleidoscope Paints Limited showcased his astute understanding of the significance of a brand's name in creating a unique market identity. His grasp on this concept was seemingly ahead of his time and has become even more critical in today's digital age, where the brand name carries immense weight in driving customer engagement.

Parson's approach to overcoming challenges was rooted in optimism and resilience, a quality that resonates profoundly with entrepreneurs facing the volatility of today's market conditions. His ability to convert opposition into opportunities, as seen with his former employer Berger Trinidad, exemplifies a mindset that sees obstacles as steppingstones to success.

Stephen Sonny Parson was undoubtedly an entrepreneur ahead of his time. His principles and strategies reflect modern entrepreneurial practices, underscoring his visionary prowess. His journey from an administrative assistant to a pioneering business figure in the Caribbean paints an awe-inspiring narrative of perseverance and visionary entrepreneurship. Parson's life offers invaluable lessons for contemporary and future entrepreneurs: success is not measured merely by monetary gain, but by the legacy we leave behind. It is this legacy of Parson's entrepreneurial spirit that continues to reverberate within the vibrant walls of Kaleidoscope Paints Limited and beyond. His life story is indeed a canvas of triumph over adversity, a testament to the power of belief, integrity, and undying entrepreneurial spirit.

Overview:

Chapter 15 explores the legacy of Stephen Sonny Parson, highlighting his entrepreneurial journey as a tapestry of perseverance, innovation, and leadership. Parson's vision and drive led to the creation of Kaleidoscope Paints Limited (KPL), an enterprise that represents his unwavering commitment and entrepreneurial acumen. Parson's forward-thinking mindset, collaborative approach, and understanding of branding further demonstrate his visionary prowess.

Key Points:

1. Visionary entrepreneurship: Parson's vision and drive led to the creation of KPL, reflecting his commitment to impactful change.
2. Effective resource utilization: Parson effectively utilized available resources, transforming barren lands into a thriving factory.
3. Integrity and transparency: Parson's commitment to integrity and transparency in business dealings aligns with contemporary entrepreneurial practices.
4. People-centric leadership: Parson's faith in human potential and the integral role his family played in the company's growth align with a people-centric approach in modern businesses.
5. Strategic partnerships: Parson's collaborative approach and alliances with influential professionals reflect the importance of strategic partnerships in today's entrepreneurial landscape.
6. Branding and market identity: Parson's understanding of the significance of branding and the name change to KPL showcases his visionary approach and the relevance of brand identity in the digital age.

Chapter 16

Triumphs and Tribulations

"Every artist dips his brush in his own soul, and paints his own nature into his pictures." – Jackie Hinkson

Stephen Sonny Parson's life was a beacon of resilience and dedication. The trials he faced and the triumphs he secured were closely interwoven, painting a portrait of a man whose strength of character was matched only by his indefatigable spirit. His journey was marked by tireless dedication, a quality that steered his company, Kaleidoscope Paints Limited, through various challenges, towards steady growth.

When most people find themselves comfortably settling into the rhythm of life, Stephen was confronted with a life-altering experience. He suffered a heart attack, a cruel reminder of the toll his relentless commitment to work had taken on his health. This event marked a dramatic turning point in Stephen's life and career, challenging his grit and endurance. It was an instance that demonstrated that success often comes at a high price.

Despite the severe health setback, Stephen's spirit remained unbroken. After a period of recovery, he chose not merely to return to work, but to continue leading his business with the same fervor as before. Even when faced with successive health challenges, his commitment to his work remained undeterred. His fortitude in the face of adversity offered a stirring lesson in resilience and dedication, reinforcing his image as a steadfast leader.

Amid the turbulence, Stephen managed to remain grounded. He retained his kind-hearted nature, never allowing the stress of his professional life to overshadow his personal responsibilities. As a compassionate employer, he was ever mindful of his employees' welfare, recognizing their role in his company's success. He understood that his enterprise was more than just a business; it was a collective endeavor, and each employee's wellbeing was integral to its overall health.

Equally, he never lost sight of his duties as a family man. His commitment to his wife, children, and extended family remained unwavering, showing that while his work was his passion, his family was his anchor. Stephen's ability to balance his professional and personal life, despite his health issues, added a remarkable dimension to his life's narrative.

Stephen's life was an embodiment of triumph against odds. Despite the trials he faced, he stayed committed to his company's vision, turning Kaleidoscope Paints Limited into a leading player in the Caribbean paint industry. His leadership ensured the company's survival and success, even as he weathered personal storms. His resolve to keep pushing forward, no matter the hurdles, served as an inspiring lesson for those around him.

This chapter of Stephen Sonny Parson's life encapsulates the essence of his character — relentless dedication, resilience in the face of adversity, and the ability to keep personal and professional commitments in harmony. His tale is not just one of success, but of the trials that often accompany such success, and the triumphant spirit that sees through these trials. Even as his health faltered, his spirit remained strong, providing a powerful testament to his extraordinary strength and resolve.

Overview:

Chapter 16 delves into the remarkable resilience and dedication of Stephen Sonny Parson in the face of trials and triumphs. His unwavering commitment to his company, Kaleidoscope Paints Limited, steered it through challenges and ensured steady growth. A life-altering heart attack became a turning point, testing his grit and endurance. Despite health setbacks, Stephen's spirit remained unbroken, and he continued leading his business with fervor. His fortitude in the face of adversity showcased his resilience and dedication, solidifying his image as a steadfast leader. Despite personal and professional challenges, he maintained compassion as an employer and a strong commitment to his family.

Key Points:

1. Resilience and dedication: Stephen's journey exemplifies unwavering commitment and resilience in the face of challenges.
2. Turning point: A life-altering heart attack marked a dramatic turning point in Stephen's life and career.
3. Leadership through adversity: Stephen's commitment to his work remained undeterred, even in the face of successive health challenges.
4. Compassionate employer: He prioritized the welfare of his employees, recognizing their importance in the company's success.
5. Balancing personal and professional life: Stephen remained committed to his family, demonstrating the ability to balance personal and professional responsibilities.
6. Triumph against odds: His leadership ensured Kaleidoscope Paints Limited's survival and success despite personal trials.

Chapter 17

Final Days

"The Lord is my shepherd, I shall not want. He makes me lie down in green pastures; He leads me beside the still waters. He restores my soul; He leads me in the paths of righteousness for His name's sake. Yea though I walk through the valley of the shadow of death, I will fear no evil, for You are with me; Your rod and Your staff, they comfort me. You prepare a table before me in the presence of my enemies; You anoint my head with oil; my cup overflows. Surely goodness and mercy will follow me all the days of my life; And I will dwell in the house of the Lord forever."- Psalms 23

The final chapter in the life of Stephen Sonny Parson was marked by an abrupt conclusion that was as unexpected as it was impactful. During the two decades of his suffering from heart disease, Stephen worked eighteen (18) hours a day and more seven days a week until he fell ill in 1982. At this time, he had a double bypass operation. Against his doctor's instructions, Stephen shortly begun working long hours again until he had neurosurgery in November 1984, as well as multiple heart attacks during this period.

Remarkably, even by 1986, five (5) years prior to his passing, Stephen never took his annual vacation leave, displaying his unwavering dedication and an unparalleled sense of commitment. His refusal to break away from the intense work rhythm symbolized his unyielding dedication to his company and the mission it represented. This level of devotion continued to define him right until the end, a testament to his unshakeable resolve and his exceptional character.

Stephen's sudden death on September 9th, 1991, a mere two days after his youngest daughter's wedding, sent a ripple of shock through his family and the broader community. Yet, in the face of this abrupt loss, the unity that Stephen had fostered within his family became their beacon, guiding them through the grief and uncertainty that followed. Stephen's funeral took place on September 12th, 1991.

The legacy that Stephen left behind was multifaceted and profound. His personal values of ambition, resilience, and a deep sense of responsibility, carefully imparted to his children and grandchildren, continue to echo in their lives decades after his passing. These values are not just principles they live by but are the foundational stones of their personal and professional endeavors, ensuring Stephen's influence lives on in each successive generation.

Stephen's business acumen, displayed through the growth and success of Kaleidoscope Paints Limited, has survived him and continues to make waves in the Caribbean paint industry. From a humble start on a plot of land measuring five thousand (5,000) square feet, the company has evolved into an industry leader with a sprawling manufacturing plant and multiple retail outlets spread across Trinidad and Tobago. Stephen's vision, embedded in the company's DNA, is continually upheld by his descendants who run the business with the same relentless dedication he exemplified.

His impact extended beyond the realm of business, touching the lives of everyday people in Trinidad and Tobago. The homes and businesses adorned with Kaleidoscope Paints tell the story of a local enterprise that has become part of the fabric of the nation. Through the reach of his company, Stephen's legacy permeates the islands, embodying the spirit of a man who once dreamt of providing quality paint solutions for his people.

A pillar of his community, Stephen's commitment to his faith was a significant part of his legacy. He was deeply engaged with the Presbyterian Church of Trinidad and Tobago, contributing to its development and community programs. Today, the church remembers Stephen as a paragon of faith and spirit, a testament to his enduring influence on the community that he loved and served. Stephen Sonny Parson was not a mere businessman.

His life was a masterful symphony of varied roles— a successful entrepreneur, a devoted family man, a faith-driven community leader— each played with sincerity and dedication. His story, marked by sacrifice, resilience, and love, serves as a guiding light for those who knew him and for many who have come to know of him posthumously.

Today, as his family, the company he built, and the community he significantly influenced move forward, they carry with them the essence of Stephen Sonny Parson. His memory continues to inspire, reminding all of the values he held dear and the dreams he worked tirelessly to achieve. Stephen's life story is not simply one of success or overcoming adversity, but of a man's enduring spirit shaping an enduring legacy. His narrative continues to motivate, influence, and provide a blueprint of aspiration, resilience, and love.

Overview:

Chapter 17 concludes Stephen Sonny Parson's biography with the sudden and impactful end of his life. His sudden death left his family and the community in shock, but the unity he fostered within his family became their guiding light through grief and uncertainty. Stephen's legacy was multifaceted, extending beyond his business success. The values he imparted to his children and grandchildren continue to shape their lives, while Kaleidoscope Paints Limited thrives as an industry leader, carrying on his vision. His impact on the community and his commitment to faith are remembered and cherished.

Key Points:

1. Sudden loss: Stephen's unexpected death sent shockwaves through his family and community.
2. Unity in grief: The unity Stephen fostered within his family became their strength during a challenging time.
3. Lasting legacy: His personal values of ambition, resilience, and responsibility continue to influence subsequent generations.
4. Business success: Kaleidoscope Paints Limited thrives as an industry leader, upholding Stephen's vision.
5. Impact on the community: The company's reach extends to homes and businesses across Trinidad and Tobago, becoming part of the nation's fabric.
6. Commitment to faith: Stephen's involvement in the Presbyterian Church of Trinidad and Tobago is remembered as a testament to his enduring influence.
7. A life of varied roles: Stephen's life encompassed being an entrepreneur, family man, and community leader with dedication and sincerity.

CHAPTER 18

THROUGH THE EYES OF THE ELDER BROTHER: THE BLOSSOMING OF PARSAN'S FAMILY

"Today's accomplishments were yesterday's impossibilities."
– Robert Schuller

The journey of Parsan's family blossomed like a tree, stretching its roots and branches to cultivate a rich legacy. The household, once an intimate group of three, grew exponentially under the guidance of patriarch, Parsan, and matriarch, Sancharie, whose love and toil nurtured a family that expanded beyond the humble confines of its beginnings.

There were fourteen children, a merry band that filled the home with love and laughter. Each child carried a fragment of Parsan and Sancharie within them, including the youngest - a resilient, visionary individual – Stephen Sonny Parson.

Born into this rich tapestry of familial bonds, Stephen Sonny Parson, was the embodiment of entrepreneurship and fortitude. Navigating through life, his entrepreneurial journey was not an isolated saga but was intrinsically intertwined with his roots, with his sprawling family serving as the compass that guided his path.

Tracing Stephen's footsteps against the backdrop of his family history, we can appreciate Stephen's family-oriented nature as well as his remarkable communication skills, which would assist him in his later years in running his business. He grew up witnessing the expansion of his family, from the original cluster of sixteen (16), into an assembly of a whopping ninety-four (94) members. If Stephen's uncle, Parsotum, and grandmother, Bachni, are included, the family spans a total of ninety-six (96) members which arose from the original group of three (3) that came to Trinidad on November 12th, 1896, from India. Each of Parsan's fourteen (14) children introduced a new set of individuals into the family - spouses and children, with a total of fourteen (14) spouses and sixty-four (64) children, enriching the collective heritage.

From each union and each birth, there were new stories, new dreams, and new hopes, much like the entrepreneurial ventures that Stephen would later nurture. The lesson was clear: growth requires embracing change, welcoming new members, and adapting to new circumstances - a lesson that Stephen translated to his entrepreneurial ventures.

Stephen's family's growth mirrored his entrepreneurial growth - dynamic, expansive, and encompassing a multitude of individuals with diverse talents and aspirations. Much like modern entrepreneurial strategies emphasize the importance of diversity, innovation, and adaptability, Stephen's business approach was shaped by these principles long before they became the norm. He was, in many ways, a man ahead of his time.

However, growth was not the only shared experience between his family life and his entrepreneurial journey. Stephen was the youngest of Parsan's fourteen children. As Stephen navigated life, he faced the inevitable sorrow of losing family members, his siblings passing away one after the other, marking the end of an era. At the age of six (6), Stephen lost his older sister.

When Stephen was just twenty-two (22), he lost his older brother of forty (40) years. His older brother, who had embraced family life with seven (7) children and a wife, mirrored the complexity and diversity of a thriving enterprise. His passing demonstrated the transient nature of life, a reality that would echo throughout Stephen's journey in the business world.

Then, when Stephen was twenty-four (24), his mother Sancharie passed away, at the age of sixty-four (64) years. The loss was substantial, but the teachings from his mother lived on within him. They instilled a sense of endurance that would later become the cornerstone of his entrepreneurial endeavors.

Six (6) years later, at the age of thirty (30), his father, Parsan, passed away, at the age of seventy-three (73), marking the end of an era. The patriarch's death left a permanent impact on Stephen, reminding him of the cycle of life and the imperative to leave a lasting legacy.

Throughout the 60s and 70s, Stephen experienced the passing of more of his older siblings. These included his two older siblings, at the ages of fifty-five (55) and sixty-four (64). With each loss, Stephen's resilience was tested and honed. Yet, as in business, he understood that trials and tribulations are part and parcel of life. The resilience he learned during these times helped him navigate through the vicissitudes of the business world.

As the 80s rolled around, Stephen lost five more siblings, two siblings at the ages of sixty-five (65), one sibling at the age of fifty-one (51), a further sibling at the age of sixty-two (62), and another at the age of fifty-seven (57), while navigating the tumultuous business landscape. The deaths of family members were like unexpected market shifts or business failures. But with every loss, Stephen, like a seasoned entrepreneur, learned to adapt, innovate, and persevere. In the 90s, his older sister passed away, at the age of seventy-six (76). By the time Stephen himself passed away in 1991 at the age of fifty-six (56), he had lived through the passing of his parents, ten (10) of his siblings, four (4) of his sisters-in-law, and four (4) of Parsan's grandchildren. These experiences, while heartbreaking, underscored the importance of resilience, adaptability, and the continuous pursuit of growth - values he brought into his entrepreneurial endeavors.

Just as the family tree continued to grow, despite the loss of its branches, Stephen's entrepreneurial ventures continued to expand, demonstrating the same resilience and commitment. The deaths of his siblings, though painful, provided a profound lesson: losses do not signify the end, but rather herald the beginning of new chapters. This perspective on life and business was not just inspiring but revolutionary.

The story of Stephen Sonny Parson is not just about a man who built a thriving empire. It is a testament to the rich familial legacy that served as the foundation for his ventures. It is about a man who imbibed lessons from his personal life, translating them into a distinctive entrepreneurial philosophy that was progressive, resilient, and impactful.

The tale of Stephen's life serves as an inspiration, a reminder of the potential each one of us holds within ourselves to change our narrative and leave an ineradicable mark on the world. His life encourages us to dream, to dare, and above all, to defy the odds.

Overview:

Chapter 18 delves into the profound influence of Stephen Sonny Parson's family on his entrepreneurial journey. The chapter highlights the expansion of Parsan's family, with its roots extending from three individuals to a large and diverse collective. The growth and diversity within his family mirrored Stephen's entrepreneurial approach, emphasizing the importance of embracing change, welcoming new members, and adapting to new circumstances. The chapter also explores the inevitable losses Stephen experienced, including the passing of his siblings, which taught him resilience and endurance. These personal experiences became the cornerstone of his entrepreneurial endeavors, reminding him of the transient nature of life and the imperative to leave a lasting legacy.

Key Points:

1. Parsan's family, under the guidance of patriarch, Parsan, and matriarch, Sancharie, expanded exponentially from its humble beginnings, nurturing a rich legacy.
2. Stephen Sonny Parson, born into this family, was influenced by its growth, diversity, and familial bonds throughout his entrepreneurial journey.
3. Stephen's family expanded from the original cluster of three to a group of ninety-six (96) members, including spouses and children.
4. Growth and embracing change were shared experiences between Stephen's family life and entrepreneurial journey.
5. Stephen's resilience was tested and honed through the inevitable losses of his siblings, mirroring the trials and tribulations of the business world.

6. Each loss taught Stephen the importance of adapting, innovating, and persevering, echoing the challenges faced by entrepreneurs in a dynamic market.
7. Stephen's perspective on loss as a beginning of new chapters reflected his resilience, adaptability, and commitment to continuous growth.
8. The expansion and losses in Parsan's family served as a profound lesson for Stephen, shaping his entrepreneurial philosophy of embracing change, resilience, and pursuit of growth.
9. Stephen's entrepreneurial ventures, like the family tree, continued to expand and demonstrate resilience despite losses.
10. The story of Stephen Sonny Parson is not just about building a thriving empire but a testament to the rich familial legacy that influenced his ventures.

Chapter 19

Stephen Sonny Parson: A Love Story that Shaped an Entrepreneur

"Tough times never last, but tough people do." – Robert Schuller

Monica's voice trembled as she shared memories of the tough times that coincided with the strengthening bond between her and Stephen Sonny Parson. The tale, as melancholic as it may seem, reveals the intricate weaving of hardship, love, and a spirit that would, in time, become the foundational pillars of a successful entrepreneurial journey.

In their earlier years, as Stephen Sonny Parson was transitioning from elementary to secondary school, an endearing love story started to unfold. A story that played a significant role in shaping the entrepreneur we celebrate today. Monica, who would later become his wife, provides an intimate account of their early interactions.

Monica, who attended elementary school up until standard five, fondly remembers Stephen coming to her yard to pick up his bicycle. The family lived close by, and her stepfather often borrowed Stephen's bike to get around. Riding up to the Croisee, then up to San Juan Hill was the daily norm for school-goers. Amidst this shared routine, the seeds of a beautiful relationship were sown. Monica, although unaware at the time, was the driving force behind Stephen's frequent visits.

Though he was only in his teenage years, Stephen showcased an early trait of entrepreneurs - an understanding of value and purpose. He noticed Monica's stepsiblings needed help with their homework, and without being asked, took it upon himself to provide support. In a time where resources were scarce, Stephen's initiative reflected the proactive problem-solving characteristic seen in today's entrepreneurs.

Monica's house became a regular stop for Stephen, not only for his bicycle but also for offering help to Monica's stepsiblings. His kindness and sense of responsibility, even as a young man, were profound. Today, these attributes are recognized as integral to entrepreneurial leadership, emphasizing not just business outcomes but also personal and societal contributions. His empathetic and service-oriented approach demonstrates a social entrepreneurship aspect, an idea prevalent in today's successful business models, reflecting societal benefits alongside financial gains.

As time went on, it became evident that Stephen's afternoon visits had another purpose - he had developed an affection for Monica. The prevailing conventions in their era meant that expressing these feelings directly to Monica was not customary. Instead, Stephen's feelings were subtly conveyed, often through letters concealed in books left on Monica's banister.

Stephen's quiet pursuit of Monica reflects an important entrepreneurial lesson- persistence. His patience and continuous effort to win Monica's heart mirror an entrepreneur's journey towards building a successful business. It's rarely about quick wins but consistent and strategic actions over time.

As Monica's family dealt with a tumultuous period - Monica's mother separating from her abusive stepfather, struggling to provide for her children - Stephen was a constant figure. The absence of Monica's stepfather who gambled away his earnings, leaving the family in scarcity, was a significant blow. Monica's uncle, working as a trucker delivering goods to grocery stores, stepped in to help, but the situation remained challenging. Stephen, ever the empathetic figure, provided much-needed stability.

A significant change happened in Monica's life around the time she was turning twelve, a change that was instrumental in shaping her future. Following the departure of Monica's stepfather, her family had to find ways to sustain themselves. Monica's mother found solace and support in the community, given a table at the Port of Spain market to sell vegetables and supplies, provided by a kind neighbor. Her mother's determination in the face of adversity, paying back the debts from her sales, is an early lesson in resourcefulness and financial management.

It was then that she became the caregiver of her home and the six children. Her mother's early market trips and late returns meant Monica was responsible for running the household, mirroring the multitasking demands entrepreneurs often face.

A turn of fate occurred when Monica's mother fell gravely ill and passed away at a young age, leaving Monica and the six children orphaned. Amidst this grief, Monica's engagement to Stephen offered a ray of hope. Born into a family of devout Christians, Monica found solace and support in Stephen albeit sharing a differing faith. Their engagement was a testament to Stephen's firm conviction and the understanding nature of his family.

Despite the religious and cultural differences, with Stephen's family being staunch Hindus and Monica's family, Christians, their union was accepted with open arms by Stephen's parents, showcasing a forward-thinking attitude prevalent in Stephen's life and embodying the concept of unity in diversity, mirroring a fundamental entrepreneurial quality – openness to diversity and change.

While the familial harmony in accepting their union was heartening, Monica and Stephen faced an immense challenge. After her mother's death, Monica's uncle suggested dividing her six stepsiblings amongst the family. However, none of the family members stepped forward. This standstill moment was fortunately disrupted by Stephen's decisiveness, declaring that they would marry and take care of all six children. This significant decision could be considered the birth of his entrepreneurial spirit. In modern times, we encourage entrepreneurs to embrace challenges and obstacles as opportunities for growth. Stephen embodied this long before it became a popular mantra.

Stephen's decision to stand up for Monica and his future siblings-in-law, accepting the responsibility of an entire family, resonated deeply with the essence of his entrepreneurial spirit. It showed courage, a sense of responsibility, and the willingness to face the challenge head-on, qualities that are crucial to any successful entrepreneur.

Their journey was not easy. From being a diligent employee at British Paints to establishing Kaleidoscope Paints Limited, Stephen's path was riddled with numerous obstacles. Each hurdle only fortified his resolve. He understood the importance of a robust support system and involved his children in his business endeavors. This is reminiscent of the modern concept of 'intrapreneurship', where employees are encouraged to take ownership of their work, nurturing an entrepreneurial spirit within an existing organization. Stephen was already practicing this contemporary business strategy, once again highlighting his progressive mindset.

By involving his family in his business, he ensured that his entrepreneurial legacy would continue. His eldest daughter became a chemist, specializing in paint production. His next two daughters took on roles in accounting and administrative work, while his son delved into sales. Each child made a unique contribution to KPL, which continues to be an essential aspect of its success today.

Stephen's commitment to his family and his business took a toll on his health, leading to a heart attack and subsequent open-heart surgery, followed by brain surgery. However, these trials did not diminish his indomitable spirit. Just as modern entrepreneurs are admired for their tenacity and resilience, Stephen showcased these qualities in abundance.

The untimely death of Stephen was a colossal loss for the Parson family and the KPL family. However, his principles and vision lived on through his children. His children displayed the same entrepreneurial spirit, humbly refusing to sit in their father's chair as a mark of respect. His children's decision reflects an essential tenet of entrepreneurship – humility. In the face of success, staying grounded is as important as the courage to dream.

Reflecting on this journey, it is evident how Stephen's early life experiences significantly influenced his entrepreneurial journey. From the mundane sharing of a bicycle to the substantial act of helping Monica's family during tough times, each experience helped shape his values as a family man.

This chapter in Stephen's life, dealing with adversity and maintaining his focus on his relationship with Monica and her family, demonstrates resilience a sense of responsibility, and ability to find innovative solutions - a fundamental trait of entrepreneurship. Just as businesses face unexpected challenges, Stephen's experience provided a lesson in maintaining purpose amidst turmoil. These traits would later manifest in his successful venture, Kaleidoscope Paints Limited.

Stephen Sonny Parson's life story, as narrated by his beloved wife, Monica, is a compelling narrative of resilience, familial duty, and forward-thinking entrepreneurship. He navigated numerous challenges to build a thriving business while simultaneously managing a large family. His journey serves as an inspiration, illustrating that with dedication, hard work, and a sense of responsibility, one can indeed balance personal and professional life successfully, even in the face of adversity.

This love story, intertwined with entrepreneurial lessons, adds an enriching dimension to Stephen Sonny Parson's biography, presenting him as a man who was not just a successful entrepreneur, but also an individual who lived life with deep empathy and kindness. Stephen's life and work truly represent the spirit of entrepreneurship, making him a timeless figure of inspiration.

Overview:

Chapter 19 explores the profound love story between Stephen and Monica, highlighting the challenges they faced and the resilience and entrepreneurial spirit that emerged from their journey. The chapter reveals how Stephen's early interactions with Monica, his proactive problem-solving, and his empathetic nature laid the foundation for their relationship. Despite cultural and religious differences, Stephen's unwavering support for Monica and her family showcased his entrepreneurial qualities of courage, responsibility, and the ability to embrace challenges. Stephen's involvement of his family in his business, his commitment to their well-being, and his determination in the face of health issues exemplify the principles of intrapreneurship and resilience. Their story serves as a testament to the power of love, resilience, and entrepreneurial spirit in overcoming adversity and building a successful business.

Key Points:

1. Stephen and Monica's love story began in their teenage years, intertwining with their journey of personal and entrepreneurial growth.
2. Stephen's early interactions with Monica demonstrated entrepreneurial traits of proactive problem-solving and understanding value and purpose.
3. Stephen's regular visits to Monica's house reflected his empathetic and service-oriented approach, resembling the concept of social entrepreneurship.
4. Stephen's quiet pursuit of Monica and his consistent efforts to win her heart illustrate the importance of persistence in entrepreneurship.

5. The challenges faced by Monica's family, such as her mother's illness and financial struggles, provided early lessons in resourcefulness and financial management.
6. Monica's role as the caregiver of her home and the six children mirrored the multitasking demands often faced by entrepreneurs.
7. Despite cultural and religious differences, Stephen's family embraced their union, showcasing an openness to diversity and change.
8. Stephen's decision to take responsibility for Monica and the six children exemplified his familial spirit of facing challenges head-on and accepting responsibility.
9. Stephen's involvement of his family in his business and their unique contributions embody the principles of intrapreneurship and humility in entrepreneurship.
10. Stephen's health challenges and resilience mirror the tenacity and resilience admired in modern entrepreneurs.
11. The untimely death of Stephen marked a significant loss, but his principles and vision lived on through his children, reflecting the importance of staying grounded and humble.
12. Stephen's early life experiences significantly influenced his entrepreneurial journey, showcasing resilience, responsibility, and innovative problem-solving.
13. Stephen's love story with Monica demonstrates the ability to maintain purpose amidst adversity, a crucial trait in entrepreneurship.
14. The chapter presents Stephen Sonny Parson as a man who not only built a successful business but also lived a life of empathy, kindness, and deep love.
15. Stephen's journey serves as an inspiration, highlighting the balance between personal and professional life and the ability to overcome challenges with dedication and hard work.

Chapter 20

A Labor of Love - An Ode to Stephen Sonny Parson by his Siblings-in-Law

"Love is patient, love is kind. It does not envy, it does not boast, it is not proud. It does not dishonor others, it is not self-seeking, it is not easily angered, it keeps no record of wrongs. Love does not delight in evil but rejoices with the truth. It always protects, always trusts, always hopes, always perseveres. Love never fails."
– 1 Corinthians 13:4-8

In the nostalgic neighborhood nestled down the Eastern Main Road, a young man, Stephen Sonny Parson, commonly known by his siblings-in-law as their "brother and father," was weaving an inspiring tale. It was here, among the pastures and gardens, where he first sowed the seeds of his future enterprise, and met his future wife, Monica. In this chapter, his siblings-in-law unveil the shades of their brother's life, the brilliance of his entrepreneurial spirit, and the impact of his vision on their lives.

Stephen's entrepreneurial journey was already in bloom during his adolescence. He reared cows and gardened with his brothers, selling the milk in handbags via bicycle to earn a living. This humble beginning not only showcased his innate entrepreneurial knack but also mirrored the modern startup culture that values starting small and embracing organic growth.

Stephen first encountered Monica, who lived down the road, during his milk-selling rounds. A glance was all it took for love to blossom. His determined approach to courtship reflected the discipline and persistence that he later exhibited in his entrepreneurial pursuits.

Much like the determination required to succeed in modern business landscapes, Stephen's approach to courtship was intentional and focused.

Stephen's compassion was on full display when Monica's mother died, and her family planned to scatter her stepsiblings among different relatives. Not willing to let the family separate, Stephen boldly decided to marry Monica and take care of her six stepsiblings. His resolution to keep the family intact was akin to today's entrepreneurs who prioritize their team's unity and emotional well-being.

His brilliance became even more apparent when he used to help his future stepsiblings with their schoolwork. This foreshadowed his knack for leadership and teaching, which he later demonstrated as a business owner by guiding and mentoring his employees, a trait much admired in modern leadership principles.

The Parson household thrived under Stephen's fatherhood, guided by strict discipline and cleanliness, reflecting his personal ethos of orderliness and precision. These principles would later become the bedrock of his business, mirroring modern entrepreneurs who advocate for efficiency and structure in their enterprises.

In the humble backdrop of their home, Stephen Sonny Parson and his brothers-in-law demonstrated an unwavering entrepreneurial spirit. Their shared passion for craftsmanship was made manifest in the simple, yet lovingly constructed, household items they fashioned together. From benches to tables to shelves, Stephen's hands skillfully molded raw material into tangible, functional pieces, each a testament to his resourceful nature. Stephen's drive to create, combined with a willingness to engage external talent where his abilities fell short, hinted at his entrepreneurial acumen that was yet to be fully realized.

A sense of homeliness was fostered in the Parson household through their tradition of rearing farm animals. An assortment of goats, chickens, and turkeys constituted a small, albeit lively, menagerie that was part of their daily life. As Stephen's brother-in-law recounted, life was abundant, and their time together was filled with vibrant colors, much like a kaleidoscope.

One of the most vivid memories of Stephen involves him bringing paint cans home and the ensuing hilarity of getting paint all over themselves. There was a certain infectious enthusiasm about Stephen as he painted their house, translating into a hands-on learning experience for his brother-in-law. Such instances are reminiscent of present-day entrepreneurs who are passionate about their craft, unafraid of getting their hands dirty.

Stephen was also a committed family man, frequently taking his loved ones for outings by the river. These excursions provided the perfect balance of relaxation and bonding time, painting a picture of Stephen as a man of robust work-life balance, something much admired in successful entrepreneurs today.

Stephen's career in the paint industry started with British Paints. His dedication and thrift resulted in him buying his own car. His transition from a bicycle to a car parallels his personal journey of growth and prosperity. His subsequent decision to build his own company, Kaleidoscope Paints Limited, marked a significant shift in his professional trajectory. Stephen's vision for starting his factory, a testament to his pioneering mindset, mirrored the drive of modern entrepreneurs who identify gaps in their industries and seize the opportunity to fill them.

Following his departure from British Paints, where Stephen had gained invaluable experience, he saw an opportunity to venture into the paint industry independently. The decision to establish his own company did not come out of necessity but rather from a profound sense of purpose and conviction. Stephen's siblings-in-life observed how the lessons he learned from his mentor at British Paints had a profound impact on his entrepreneurial journey.

They reminisce about Stephen's decision, one that mirrors the actions of many modern-day entrepreneurs who seize opportunities amidst adversity. Stephen's bold move to establish KPL echoes the modern entrepreneurial ethos of identifying gaps in the market and innovating to fill them.

The inception of Kaleidoscope Paints was not without its trials. Stephen and his brother-in-law labored arduously, hand-mixing cement and preparing the grounds. They were the company's cornerstone, responsible for setting up the foundation and onboarding the necessary manpower.

Starting with a simple black emulsion, the product line expanded gradually to encompass a range of colors. Despite Stephen's humble beginnings and the initial lack of brand awareness, the company flourished under Stephen's determined leadership. This relentless drive reflects an entrepreneurial tenet where steadfast belief in one's product is crucial in the face of skepticism. Stephen also strived to involve the family in his business venture which is represented by the company's first jingle, produced by his siblings-in-law.

The company's initial growth, marked by strenuous work hours and late-night home drops for employees, is indicative of the sacrifices entrepreneurs often need to make toward achieving the pinnacle of success. This unfaltering dedication to his dream and his workforce showcased Stephen's commitment and empathy, a combination that sets apart inspiring leaders.

Stephen also implemented engaging employee practices, including monthly birthday parties and regular team outings. Such activities fostered a sense of camaraderie and family within the company. This focus on employee engagement and happiness mirrors the ethos of many modern, successful businesses, demonstrating Stephen's forward-thinking leadership style.

Even as Kaleidoscope Paints Limited underwent its numerous expansions, there were lighter moments that served as a reminder of the human element behind the scenes. One such incident that stands out is when a bee nest, nestled within one of the trees on the KPL property, was unwittingly dislodged by a tractor during construction. What ensued was a chaotic, yet humorous scene as people scampered for cover, dodging the disgruntled swarm. This fond recollection was an unexpected interruption to the business of the day, with workers seeking refuge in the most unlikely hiding spots.

This anecdote, while providing a dose of comic relief, also underscores the shared experiences that often accompany ventures of such magnitude. It serves as a reminder that, even in the throes of expansion and pursuit of business success, there are moments of unexpected levity that contribute to the richness of the entrepreneurial journey.

However, Stephen's journey was not devoid of challenges. He faced stiff competition, product recalls, quality issues, water shortages, and even fires. Despite these obstacles, his resilience shone through, prompting continuous improvement and innovation. His decision to install water tanks to combat water shortages showcases his adaptability and problem-solving skills, qualities that are prized in the entrepreneurial world today.

Kaleidoscope Paints Limited's steady rise to prominence was further bolstered by its successful expansion into the export market. However, this progress came with its own set of hurdles, including product quality issues and balancing the workload. Nevertheless, Stephen's commitment to quality and growth never wavered.

Stephen's gentle yet firm nature as a family man reflected his leadership style in his business. His quiet intelligence, fairness, and respect for everyone were echoed in his managerial style, aligning with modern entrepreneurial strategies that emphasize empathy and respectful communication.

A testament to his astute devotion to his wife and family was Stephen's decision to convert to Christianity from a strong Hindu background. As KPL began to take shape, Stephen's wife noticed another aspect of her husband's personality that deeply touched her - his generosity. Stephen embodied the spirit of corporate social responsibility long before it became a mainstream concept in the business world. Every Christmas, Stephen would host a grand party at KPL for the local children. Word of this annual celebration, filled with Christmas goodies, spread beyond their locality of San Juan, attracting children from as far as Curepe and Tunapuna.

Stephen's philanthropic tradition, a testament to his love for community and people, would attract about a thousand children annually, a testament to his large heart. His generosity is reminiscent of many modern corporations that embed giving back to society into their business models, highlighting his visionary outlook.

Stephen Sonny Parson was not just an entrepreneur; he was a community leader and a beacon of generosity. He understood that the success of a company was intrinsically tied to the community it serves. This belief in creating a symbiotic relationship between a business and its community is a principle that modern entrepreneurs are increasingly embracing.

Stephen was not just an entrepreneur; he was a visionary. His ideas for expansion, such as a balloon business, demonstrate a mindset that is not just reactive but proactive, a trait that distinguishes successful entrepreneurs today. Despite his untimely death, his ambitious plans showed an enduring desire to innovate and grow, leaving a roadmap for the future of Kaleidoscope Paints Limited.

Looking back, Stephen's entrepreneurial journey seems filled with a kaleidoscope of experiences, each one more colorful than the last. From an early age, Stephen demonstrated a knack for building things, an uncanny ability to make the best use of resources, and a resilience that would carry him through the challenges of entrepreneurship. These qualities allowed him to successfully carve out a niche in a market dominated by established brands, a feat that would inspire future generations of entrepreneurs.

Stephen Sonny Parson's life, as narrated by his siblings-in-law, was a story of love, resilience, and ambition. His passion for his work, resilience in the face of adversity, care for his employees, ability to adapt to market demands, visionary thinking, entrepreneurial brilliance, and unwavering dedication to his family and his business embody the ideals of modern entrepreneurship. His legacy, therefore, serves as an inspiring tale for aspiring entrepreneurs who wish to make a difference in their communities.

Overview:

Chapter 20 unveils the formative years of Stephen's entrepreneurial journey through the perspective of his siblings-in-law. From his humble beginnings rearing cows and selling milk to his courtship and marriage to Monica, Stephen's determination, compassion, and leadership qualities shine through. The chapter highlights Stephen's resourcefulness, hands-on approach, commitment to family, and his eventual establishment of Kaleidoscope Paints Limited. His relentless drive, resilience, and vision for growth and innovation serve as an inspiration for aspiring entrepreneurs.

Key Points:

1. Stephen's entrepreneurial spirit was evident in his adolescence as he sold milk, showcasing his innate knack for business and organic growth.
2. His determined approach to courtship reflected the discipline and persistence he would later demonstrate in his entrepreneurial pursuits.
3. Stephen's decision to marry Monica and care for her six stepsiblings highlighted his compassion and commitment to keeping the family intact, mirroring the unity prioritized by modern entrepreneurs.
4. His assistance with schoolwork foreshadowed his leadership and mentoring abilities, characteristics admired in successful business owners.
5. The Parson household thrived under Stephen's fatherhood, guided by strict discipline and cleanliness, reflecting his personal ethos of orderliness and precision.
6. Stephen's resourcefulness and willingness to engage external talent in their shared craftsmanship hinted at his entrepreneurial acumen.

7. The tradition of rearing farm animals fostered a sense of homeliness and a vibrant life in the Parson household, aligning with Stephen's hands-on approach.
8. Stephen's transition from a bicycle to owning a car paralleled his personal growth and prosperity, symbolizing his evolving entrepreneurial journey.
9. The establishment of Kaleidoscope Paints Limited marked a significant shift in Stephen's professional trajectory, reflecting his visionary mindset and seizing opportunities in the industry.
10. Starting with a simple black emulsion, the company gradually expanded its product line, reflecting Stephen's steadfast belief in the face of skepticism.
11. The sacrifices made during the company's initial growth phase, along with Stephen's dedication and empathy for his workforce, demonstrated his commitment and inspiring leadership style.
12. Engaging employee practices, such as monthly birthday parties and team outings, fostered camaraderie and family-like bonds, mirroring modern successful businesses.
13. Despite challenges, including stiff competition, recalls, and water shortages, Stephen's resilience and adaptability fueled continuous improvement and innovation.
14. Expansion into the export market showcased Stephen's commitment to quality and growth, while maintaining his leadership style of fairness and respect.
15. His visionary mindset extended to ambitious plans for the future, exemplifying proactive thinking and a desire to innovate and grow.
16. Stephen's decision to establish his own company, KPL, after the closure of British Paints demonstrates his entrepreneurial drive, seizing opportunities amidst adversity.

17. His bold move reflects the modern entrepreneurial ethos of identifying market gaps and innovating to fill them.
18. The lessons Stephen learned from his mentor at British Paints influenced his entrepreneurial journey.
19. Stephen's decision to establish KPL aligns with the actions of many modern-day entrepreneurs who embark on their own ventures driven by a profound sense of purpose and conviction.
20. Stephen's generosity and embodiment of corporate social responsibility were evident in his annual Christmas party for local children at KPL.
21. Stephen's philanthropic tradition attracted about a thousand children annually, reflecting the impact of his generosity and the community's recognition of his large heart.
22. Stephen's generosity exemplifies his visionary outlook and highlights his commitment to the community.
23. Stephen's entrepreneurial journey exemplified resourcefulness, resilience, ambition, and dedication to family and business, inspiring future generations of entrepreneurs.

Chapter 21

The Firm yet Loving Guardian - Children's Account of Stephen Sonny Parson

"Old age is like everything else. To make a success of it, you've got to start young." – Theodore Roosevelt

To understand the multifaceted character of Stephen Sonny Parson, the visionary founder of Kaleidoscope Paints Limited, one must sift through the lens of his children, who paint an intricate portrait of a man who was equal parts strict, caring, and innovative. As an entrepreneur, he demonstrated a leadership style that was both authoritative and compassionate, not unlike the nuanced management strategies celebrated in the business world today. His stern, business-oriented demeanor resonated profoundly within the factory; his message was clear – factory business was factory business and home was home. There was no room for distraction or frivolity.

Stephen, known for his firm and "no-nonsense" demeanor, was deeply committed to instilling discipline and a strong work ethic in his children, traits they both admired and feared. His business strategies aligned with the modern concept of Time Management, evident in his meticulous approach to everything, from entering his office to implementing business procedures. The punctuality and work ethic that Stephen instilled in his family now permeate the company culture at Kaleidoscope Paints Limited (KPL), fostering efficiency and productivity. His commitment to setting boundaries, even within his family, mirrored the increasingly popular concept in today's business world of establishing clear and transparent guidelines for effective and efficient work processes. However, beneath his stern exterior was a well of humor and warmth that always managed to shine through, reflecting the successful entrepreneurial strategy of using humor and empathy to build stronger, more effective teams.

Despite this, Stephen demonstrated a unique balance between discipline and care that instilled a deep-seated respect in his children. The children recall an account of a desperate man seeking employment which stands as a testament to Stephen's compassionate leadership. The man, burdened by financial strain, applied for a job at the factory. Upon hearing his predicament, Stephen immediately employed him, offering a helping hand by providing an exorbitant donation. This act of generosity was etched into the man's memory, manifesting into an annual phone call to Stephen's children, a tribute to the kindness he was shown.

A testament to Stephen's sense of community and compassionate spirit was his relationship with an elderly neighbor whose house he used to walk past on his way to school. When he established his factory, he didn't forget the bonds forged during his formative years and hired his neighbor to assist with the cleaning. This was not simply an act of providing employment; it was a gesture of respect, acknowledgement, and inclusion.

Stephen was known to stand up for his neighbor whenever she faced adversity, a reflection of his inherent sense of justice. This lady, who was unique in her community, found an unwavering friend in Stephen, and their relationship depicted his extraordinary capacity for empathy, far beyond the realms of his entrepreneurial activities. This exemplifies the unique blend of compassion and astute business acumen that defined Stephen, elements that entrepreneurs today could certainly stand to emulate.

This balance of stern leadership and compassion was reflected in his approach towards his children within the factory. He introduced them to various departments, allowing them to experience the different facets of his business. This exposure wasn't just about familiarizing his children with his work; it was about imparting the virtues of hard work, discipline, and dedication.

His children recount an incident from their childhood that encapsulates Stephen's commitment to his family and his sense of justice. When a schoolteacher struck one of his children, Stephen, visibly upset, took the matter up with the school, exhibiting the same passion and protectiveness for his family that he channeled into his business. His actions that day mirror modern entrepreneurship's emphasis on ethical business practices and standing up for what's right, even in the face of adversity.

Despite his firm approach to parenting, Stephen's love, commitment, and care for his family were undeniable. Every summer, he would send his family on holidays, a practice that showcases his understanding of the importance of work-life balance, a principle that modern-day entrepreneurs are increasingly prioritizing. As an avid traveler, Stephen took his family on weekly outings as well as to places around the world, from the beaches of Maracas and Mayaro to the wonderlands of Disney World and Europe.

Stephen had a signature laugh that echoed through their home, a sound still fondly remembered by his children. He loved to party, an infectious spirit that manifested in the grand New Year's Eve parties he hosted for his family. These ventures outside of work and the balance he maintained between his business and personal life are indicative of the versatile character he embodied, fostering healthy relationships and preventing burnout. His respect for work-life boundaries was evident in his interactions with his children.

Punishments were metered out only when his wife, Monica, felt it was necessary, a clear example of his collaborative and democratic approach, valued in present-day business management.

In contrast to modern day entrepreneurial strategies, which often focus on quick expansion and high-risk investments, Stephen was guided by a sense of measured patience and wisdom. He was deeply invested in fostering a strong local community, and his annual Christmas event for children demonstrated this. Thousands of local children would flock to the Kaleidoscope Paints Factory for a Christmas treat, creating a spectacle of joy and unity. This event, as well as his routines of supporting local market vendors, showed Stephen's appreciation for his community and illustrated the value he placed on nurturing social relationships, an often-overlooked aspect of business.

Stephen's children describe him as a strict yet gentle figure who would often make jokes, balancing discipline with a lighter side. When his children opposed his views, his initial disappointment did not stop him from maintaining their relationship, demonstrating his capacity for understanding and forgiveness. This type of emotional intelligence and resilience is a core attribute of successful entrepreneurs in today's fast-paced business world.

His emphasis on hard work and dedication transcended his personal life and seeped into his professional realm. His children recollected his insistence on going to work and doing the best one could, qualities they have emulated in their own lives. His role as a "no-nonsense boss" fostered an environment of high expectations and commitment to excellence, akin to the high-performance culture prevalent in modern startups.

The impact of Stephen's teachings extended beyond just work ethics. He was meticulous about maintaining a tidy home and finishing chores before he returned from work, underscoring his commitment to orderliness and precision. These principles would later become the cornerstone of his business, reflecting the modern-day entrepreneurial emphasis on efficiency and organization.

Stephen's ambition was contagious, and he wanted his children to imbibe the same drive. His love for his family was boundless, and he yearned for everyone to share a close relationship, just as he desired his business to maintain strong relationships with its stakeholders. This aspect of Stephen's life is reminiscent of the current emphasis on stakeholder capitalism and the importance of nurturing all relationships in the business ecosystem.

Stephen skillfully balanced his personal and professional lives, a testament to his astute leadership. His children recall how Stephen always ensured that family and work remained separate entities. This clear demarcation of roles, responsibilities, and spaces is a testament to his strategic vision, reflecting the modern entrepreneurial concept of maintaining a healthy work-life balance.

His children lovingly remember his personal quirks that added charm to his rigorous personality - the joy he found in family traditions like Christmas and New Year's Eve celebrations, the pride he took in his children's accomplishments, and the little acts of kindness that filled their lives with happiness.

His passions weren't just limited to travel and parties. Stephen was a carpenter in his early years, crafting tables, benches, and cribs. This hands-on approach to creation is reminiscent of the modern 'Maker Movement' in entrepreneurship, which emphasizes the value of self-production and craftsmanship. His children would watch in fascination, playing on piles of gravel, as he sawed wood and mixed cement in the yard, suggesting that he believed in the principle of 'learning by doing', long before it was popularized in educational and business spheres.

His fondness for card games, especially with his brothers during their regular family gatherings, showed his strategic thinking and risk assessment skills - both crucial traits in successful entrepreneurs. Playing cards requires one to make calculated decisions, read the opponent, and adapt strategy as the game unfolds, much like navigating the business landscape.

His children also cherish memories of Stephen's beautiful and signature handwriting, an inerasable mark of his sophistication and brilliance as the founder of Kaleidoscope Paints Limited and as a doting father. The fluid elegance of his handwriting reflected his thoughtful and deliberate nature, qualities that permeated his approach to both business and family life. Moreover, Stephen's mastery of shorthand writing was an unusual asset, setting him apart in his time. His ability to quickly transcribe ideas and information, a skill acquired in an era when digital notetaking was unheard of, underpinned his ability to act swiftly in business matters - a trait that gave him a competitive edge in the entrepreneurial world.

Stephen's varied reading interests, including health, religion, and nutrition, indicated a mind constantly seeking knowledge and enlightenment. In today's terms, this lifelong learning mindset is regarded as an essential quality for entrepreneurs to stay ahead in rapidly evolving industries.

His food preferences revealed a man who valued simple comfort food like "dhal and rice", as well as culturally diverse cuisine like

Chinese food. This appreciation for diversity can be linked to an open-minded and inclusive business approach, traits celebrated in modern entrepreneurship.

Stephen was also a romantic, surprising his wife, Monica, on every occasion with enormous floral arrangements and bouquets of roses. This romantic side of him indicates an emotional intelligence that's highly regarded in today's leadership styles. It showcases his understanding of appreciation and the power of gestures, attributes that can translate into maintaining excellent relations with employees and partners in a business setting.

His involvement in the church's men's group showed a commitment to community, especially his presidency of the group in 1968, a trait aligning with the modern concept of Corporate Social Responsibility. His support for community events indicates his belief in giving back, a principle increasingly embedded in contemporary business practices.

Stephen's love for walks around his community and his commitment to staying active show his understanding of physical wellbeing as a crucial element for mental acuity. Today, this understanding aligns with the concept of 'Work-Life Balance' and 'Holistic Health,' crucial for entrepreneurial resilience and longevity.

A sharp dresser as well as a lover and collector of vintage and Indian music, Stephen had an affinity for exquisite clothing, accessories as well as religiously shining his shoes. Stephen took Hindi classes at the University of the West Indies in his final years, demonstrating a never-ending thirst for knowledge and a dedication to personal development. Stephen even became friends with a local prominent professor through his passion for Hindi, showcasing his knack for connections and forging relationships with new people. This balanced life approach was well ahead of its time and aligns with today's focus on work-life balance, a testament to his visionary mindset.

In the later years of his life, Stephen faced health challenges. His heart disease resulted in a shift in his routine, with him being unable to commute between home and work. During this period, his children served as his drivers, traveling across Trinidad and beyond in search of music records, players and cassettes, new business avenues as well as pursuit of his hobbies and pastimes. These shared journeys are reflective of the modern principle of 'Experiential Learning', allowing his children to learn firsthand about business operations, negotiations, and relationship-building, all the while creating lasting memories.

Despite his health difficulties, his resilience shone through. He still strived for new ventures, one of them being a balloon manufacturing unit, an idea that was later transformed into Festive Balloons by the family Board of Directors. His ability to continuously strive for growth even in challenging times exemplifies his entrepreneurial spirit and the resilience that is integral to successful entrepreneurship.

Stephen's approach to business was uncompromising, particularly when it came to quality. He diligently upheld this principle, even if it meant personally delivering a few gallons of paint to a remote hardware store. His insistence on quotations for purchases suggests his commitment to financial prudence and competitive pricing, a timeless entrepreneurial strategy.

His interaction with employees, often joining them for meals and card games, shows his belief in maintaining strong interpersonal relationships, a value that resonates with the contemporary concept of 'Emotional Intelligence.'

Stephen's unwavering focus on KPL's growth, pushing for increased sales, and strategizing to edge out competition paints a picture of a fiercely competitive entrepreneur. His decision to acquire land for business expansion signifies his visionary approach and aligns with modern entrepreneurial tactics of strategic acquisition for growth.

Stephen's stern yet empathetic approach to handling family members at work embodies his commitment to professionalism and accountability. His expectation for punctuality and proper conduct indicates a clear demarcation between familial bonds and professional duties, a strategy that aligns with modern best practices for family-run businesses.

Stephen's insistence on separating work and home life, being present in business, remaining competitive, and maintaining quality are lessons his children carried forward, embodying them in their daily routines and business decisions. This adherence to their father's teachings embodies the modern principle of 'Consistent Execution'.

The personal and professional values his children adopted from Stephen have helped them navigate through the challenging landscape of entrepreneurship. His focus on remaining humble, being intolerant of nonsense, punctuality, and commitment to his business mirror modern-day entrepreneurial best practices, illustrating the timeless relevance of Stephen's teachings.

Stephen's tradition of performing annual prayers for his family and company, a practice his children continue, showcases a unique blend of personal faith and business, a testament to the importance of tradition and belief in fostering a sense of unity and positivity within the workspace.

Stephen's succession planning, as revealed through the gifts and responsibilities at KPL left for his children, shows his acumen for forward-thinking and stability, tenets vital in contemporary business practices. Stephen's life was marked by the need to navigate personal health issues and their potential impact on his family. Following his first heart attack, he pulled key family members into the business, a strategic move that ensured continuity. This adaptive leadership strategy echoes the current entrepreneurial wisdom of having contingency plans to mitigate unexpected changes.

Stephen's conviction that practical knowledge was fundamental to leading a business resonates in today's entrepreneurial landscape. His concept of rotating leadership to avoid burnout is a forward-thinking approach to leadership, reflecting a deep understanding of the personal toll leadership can take.

Over three decades of his children's stewardship, KPL has thrived. His children believe that the company's success lies in its inorganic and organic growth strategies, a concept widely acclaimed in today's entrepreneurial world. While mergers and acquisitions have been a crucial part of the company's expansion, building a robust brand was the cornerstone of KPL's development.

Stephen had always believed in prioritizing product quality over extensive marketing. He was of the firm belief that the product should speak for itself and strongly advocated against compromising on quality. This unconventional approach allowed Stephen to reinvest the advertising budget into improving the quality of KPL's products, a strategy reminiscent of modern customer-centric businesses which focus on user experience and product quality over flashy advertising.

This investment in quality bore fruit as KPL's products gained a reputation for excellence, encouraging repeat customers and generating word-of-mouth recommendations. His children recount how Stephen took the company in a new direction when British Paints, where Stephen had formerly been employed, was sold to Berger Paints, and the quality standards declined. Unwilling to compromise, Stephen founded KPL, a 100% local, indigenous Trinidadian brand, promising to deliver superior quality paints.

His children believe that their father's entrepreneurial strategies were indeed ahead of his time. They highlight their father's decision to sponsor a local Carnival band in 1974, which was named "Kaleidoscope," as a tribute to the company. This gesture strengthened KPL's brand identity and displayed its commitment to local culture. Today, we see similar strategies being employed by modern businesses, sponsoring local talents or events as a means of building a stronger brand association and contributing to their community.

Stephen's legacy extends beyond the confines of KPL, reaching deep into the fabric of Trinidadian culture. His commitment to supporting local arts and culture was a testament to his broader vision for societal development. Today, KPL continues to uphold this tradition, ensuring its ongoing relevance and resonance in the community.

In line with today's entrepreneurial strategies, Stephen understood the importance of building strategic alliances and retaining talent to create a competitive advantage. This principle remains a cornerstone for successful businesses in the present day.

Stephen's administrative background also influenced the structural setup of KPL, with production and operations being separate from the administrative side. This foresight ensured clear delineations between the different sectors of the company, facilitating efficient operation—a model often recommended in modern business strategies.

As KPL faced early struggles, Stephen demonstrated his resilience by making unconventional decisions. Recognizing the potential in his children, he mandated their involvement in the family business. He placed each sibling where he believed their strengths lay, a management strategy widely applauded in modern entrepreneurial practices for fostering an effective team.

Stephen's eldest daughter was tasked with working in the lab—a significant responsibility. His uncompromising work ethics and rigorous expectations pushed her to learn independently, an experience she describes as stressful yet incredibly formative. His philosophy—"You had to learn to figure out things for yourself"— mirrors the modern concept of self-directed learning, often associated with entrepreneurial success.

Stephen's prioritization of education is reflected in his ambitions for his children. Stephen sent his daughter to the Netherlands to hone and develop her skills in paint manufacturing. This exposure not only broadened her understanding of paint production but also gave her international exposure—a critical aspect of entrepreneurial acumen. In the face of workforce changes, such as the departure of their first chemist, Stephen's daughter stepped up to fill the vacancy, armed with the self-teaching and experiences she had gained.

Stephen's influence in KPL extended to managing raw material purchases, a skill derived from his British Paints experience.

Following his death in 1991, his daughter seamlessly took over these responsibilities, also running the lab—a testament to her father's teachings.

As his children continue to lead KPL into the future, they reflect on their father's guiding principles. His focus on reformulating products to meet international standards reflects a modern entrepreneurial trend, highlighting sustainability and environmental consciousness, particularly through the development of low and zero Volatile Organic Compound (VOC) paints. His children's ambition to uphold KPL's commitment to quality while bringing the company's success to light reflects his dedication to his father's legacy and a vision for the future that is firmly rooted in the values that have brought them this far.

Despite their ups and downs, his children maintain that they would choose Stephen as their father over and over again. Through the lens of his children, it becomes evident that Stephen Sonny Parson was not just a brilliant entrepreneur but also a loving father, a strict disciplinarian, a caring protector, and a jovial spirit, embodying the true essence of an all-round entrepreneur who was ahead of his time.

His story serves as a beacon of inspiration for entrepreneurs who wish to excel professionally while nurturing their personal lives with equal fervor. He was more than just "The Boss"; he was a visionary, a mentor, and a symbol of entrepreneurial brilliance. His story serves as a beacon of inspiration for present and future entrepreneurs alike.

Overview:

Chapter 21 offers a unique perspective on Stephen's character through the eyes of his children. It explores his balanced leadership style, his commitment to discipline and care, and the lasting impact he had on his family and business. The chapter highlights his adherence to work-life balance, his compassion towards his employees and community, and his focus on family traditions and values. Stephen's approach to business and family exemplifies the principles of effective leadership and entrepreneurial success.

Key Points:

1. Stephen Sonny Parson was both a strict and caring father, embodying a leadership style that combined discipline and compassion.
2. His emphasis on discipline and work ethic aligned with modern concepts of Time Management and efficient work processes.
3. Stephen's ability to balance stern leadership with humor and warmth fostered strong and effective teams, reflecting contemporary entrepreneurial strategies.
4. Stephen introduced his children to different aspects of his business, instilling the virtues of hard work, discipline, and dedication.
5. His commitment to maintaining boundaries between family and work aligns with the contemporary approach of establishing clear guidelines and transparent work processes.
6. Stephen's dedication to fostering a strong local community, exemplified by the annual Christmas event for children, reflects the modern focus on community engagement and social relationships.

7. His balance of sternness and gentleness, as well as his capacity for understanding and forgiveness, demonstrates emotional intelligence and resilience, valued traits in modern leadership styles.
8. Stephen's high expectations and commitment to excellence in parenting mirrored the high-performance culture prevalent in modern startups.
9. His focus on organization and orderliness in his personal life translated into principles that became the cornerstone of his business, reflecting the modern emphasis on efficiency and organization.
10. Stephen's hands-on approach to creation, love for card games, and pursuit of knowledge through reading demonstrate qualities associated with modern entrepreneurship, such as 'learning by doing' and strategic thinking.
11. His commitment to physical and mental well-being aligns with contemporary principles of work-life balance and holistic health for entrepreneurial resilience.
12. Stephen's interest in personal development, language learning, and appreciation for diverse cultures highlight the value of continuous learning and open-mindedness in entrepreneurship.
13. His dedication to maintaining strong interpersonal relationships, as seen through his involvement in the church's Men's group, reflects the importance of emotional intelligence in modern business practices.
14. Stephen's attention to detail, financial prudence, commitment to quality, and competitive strategies exemplify timeless entrepreneurial principles for success.
15. The values and principles Stephen instilled in his children have helped them navigate the challenges of entrepreneurship and reflect the timeless relevance of his teachings.

16. Stephen's succession planning and forward-thinking strategies exemplify the importance of stability and long-term vision in contemporary business practices.
17. The success of KPL under his children's stewardship highlights the effectiveness of inorganic and organic growth strategies.
18. KPL continues to uphold this tradition, ensuring its ongoing relevance and resonance in the community.
19. Reformulating products to meet international standards, particularly in terms of sustainability and environmental consciousness, reflects a modern entrepreneurial trend.
20. The children's ambition to uphold KPL's commitment to quality while building upon their father's legacy reflects their dedication to a future rooted in the values that have brought them success.
21. Stephen Sonny Parson's relationship with a key British Paints expert during his time as an administrative assistant provided him with valuable management skills and insights into paint manufacturing.
22. Stephen developed a preference for European raw materials during his tenure at British Paints, which influenced the quality approach at KPL.
23. His partnership with a prominent chemist ensured the formulation of high-quality paints at KPL.
24. Building strategic alliances, retaining talent, and creating clear delineations between sectors were essential principles in Stephen's business strategy.
25. The structural setup of KPL, separating production and operations from the administrative side, facilitated efficient operation.
26. Stephen's unconventional decisions, such as involving his children in the family business, showcased his resilience and adaptability.

27. His philosophy of self-directed learning and sending his daughter to work in the Netherlands reflected modern entrepreneurial concepts.
28. Stephen prioritized quality over advertising, reinvesting profits to enhance product quality, aligning with present-day entrepreneurial practices.
29. Stephen's influence extended to managing raw material purchases, a skill derived from his experience at British Paints.
30. His collaborative vision for KPL involved every member of the family board of directors, emphasizing the importance of operations in driving success.
31. Stephen's conviction in the value of education and practical knowledge for leadership resonates in today's entrepreneurial landscape.

Chapter 22

The Emergence of a Paint Titan: The Formative Years from the Perspective of a Family Team Member

"The farther backward you can look, the farther forward you can see." – Winston Churchill

Stephen Sonny Parson, a man born and raised on the Eastern Main Road of Trinidad, stood as an anomaly among his siblings. Unlike them, who found their calling in the serenity of gardening, he was drawn towards a different path. He left school after marrying Monica, the love of his life and a woman with six stepsiblings to care for. Despite being offered the chance to continue his studies in England by his affluent brothers, Stephen decided to support his newfound family by finding a job, marking the initiation of an illustrious entrepreneurial journey.

This departure from the norm is indicative of the first key entrepreneurial trait that defined Parson - a willingness to take risks. In the modern entrepreneurial world, the ability to take calculated risks remains a significant characteristic. It was this quality that led him to accept a job at British Paints, a decision that would eventually carve the path for his future ventures.

His time at British Paints served as a priceless lesson, providing him a foundation in the industry that would later be indispensable. This encapsulates another crucial entrepreneurial quality that Parson embodied - learning from experiences. His belief in this principle was evident in his years of riding a bike to work, sometimes coming back for lunch, before he bought his first car. Stephen diligently worked for British Paints for several years, gaining industry knowledge and building contacts until a buy over by another company led to an exodus of the old employees. This included the chief chemist at British Paints, whose knowledge would later contribute to Stephen's venture.

When Stephen left his job at the end of 1971, it seemed like a career low-point. However, about six to eight months prior to his departure, Stephen had experienced a vision to establish his own paint company. This shows the third crucial aspect of Stephen's entrepreneurial mindset – adaptability. Modern businesses frequently laud this quality, as it allows entrepreneurs to pivot and seize new opportunities, often in times of crisis.

Stephen held a firm belief that he possessed the necessary elements to establish his own paint company. With a detailed blueprint of his operation in his mind, he plunged headfirst into the daunting task of bringing his vision to life. It was an audacious move, not unlike the bold decisions we see from contemporary disruptors in the business world. This audacity was his fourth defining trait.

Building Kaleidoscope Paints Limited was a Herculean task, made even more difficult by competing against established international players in the Caribbean paint market. However, he possessed an impressive acumen for strategy, a crucial characteristic still recognized as vital in today's entrepreneurial landscape. His strategic mind was most notably demonstrated in the way he assembled his team, where he selectively chose experienced individuals from different companies. The chief chemist, for instance, became a crucial asset. This approach enabled him to create a formidable ensemble that could navigate the intricacies of the paint industry.

Stephen's vision for his company went beyond just profitability. He believed in creating an inclusive work environment where everyone was treated like family. This approach, known in the modern business world as the 'people first approach', is increasingly recognized as a cornerstone of successful enterprises. It was this ethos that instilled a shared sense of purpose among his team, enabling them to work tirelessly, converting nights into days, to achieve their shared vision.

Stephen was also ahead of his time in terms of customer engagement. The decision to name his company 'Kaleidoscope Paints Limited' was the result of advice from an esteemed marketer. This decision indicates his early adoption of what we know today as crowd-sourcing or participatory marketing - a strategy widely used by contemporary businesses to engage customers and make them feel part of the brand.

Despite being the visionary behind the company, Stephen was not averse to accepting advice from his employees, marking his democratic and inclusive leadership style - an aspect greatly valued in modern entrepreneurship.

Stephen Sonny Parson's journey is a testament to his exceptional entrepreneurial capabilities. His willingness to take risks, learn from experiences, adapt to new circumstances, form strategic alliances, value people, and engage customers were all vital contributors to his eventual success. These elements not only set him apart in his era but would be equally commendable in the context of modern entrepreneurship. Stephen's story serves as a shining beacon of inspiration, reminding us that with the right mindset and approach, even the most daunting of goals can be achieved.

Overview:

Chapter 22 provides readers with insights into the early years of Stephen's entrepreneurial journey, as witnessed by one of his family team members. It explores Stephen's departure from the traditional path, his willingness to take risks, his dedication to learning from experiences, his adaptability, and his audacity to pursue his vision. The chapter highlights his strategic mindset, team-building abilities, inclusive leadership style, customer engagement strategies, and the values that guided him throughout his entrepreneurial endeavor.

Key Points:

1. Stephen's departure from the norm and willingness to take risks reflect crucial entrepreneurial traits valued today.
2. His time at British Paints provided valuable industry knowledge and exemplified the importance of learning from experiences.
3. Stephen's ability to adapt to changing circumstances demonstrated his entrepreneurial mindset.
4. The audacity to establish his own paint company exemplifies his bold decision-making.
5. His strategic thinking in assembling a skilled team contributed to the success of Kaleidoscope Paints Limited.
6. The 'people first approach' fostered an inclusive work environment and shared sense of purpose among the team.
7. Stephen's early adoption of customer engagement strategies, such as crowdsourcing, showcases his forward-thinking approach.
8. His democratic and inclusive leadership style valued input from employees, reflecting modern entrepreneurial principles.

Chapter 23

The Emergence of a Paint Titan: The Later Years from the Perspective of a Family Team Member

"When life seems hard, the courageous do not lie down and accept defeat; instead, they are all the more determined to struggle for a better future." – Queen Elizabeth II

In a marketplace largely dominated by local branches of multinational corporations, Stephen Sonny Parson established KPL as the first truly local paint company in Trinidad. His distinct background as the son of an indentured laborer from India lent an authentic narrative to the company's growth story. The business model was truly homegrown, akin to today's "bootstrap" startups that begin from scratch and thrive purely on determination, hard work, and an unwavering belief in the vision.

The genesis of KPL took place when Parson perceived his impending displacement from British Paints. This was when he decided to build something of his own, an entrepreneurial trigger that is often seen in the narratives of successful entrepreneurs today. Parson began the preparation for KPL's first batch of paint in October 1972, and it is awe-inspiring how family members were called upon to assist in clearing the land for the factory, demonstrating the blend of family values and business vision that is found in many successful family-owned enterprises today.

By 1981, the business venture of Stephen Sonny Parson had been functioning for nine (9) years. Although the company was a small player in the Trinidad and Tobago paint industry, Parson was unrelenting in his drive to establish a significant presence in the market. He believed that a product should be able to stand on its own two feet, with high-quality and competitive pricing as its sturdy pillars. This belief is echoed in the successful business model of Kaleidoscope Paints Limited (KPL), a company he nurtured with unwavering commitment to raw materials, quality, and word-of-mouth advertising. A series of unconventional and forward-thinking strategies would soon underscore his reputation as a visionary entrepreneur.

Despite the challenges of encouraging hardware stores to stock his paints, Parson developed a clever strategy: encouraging painters and painting contractors to purchase directly from the company. He knew that these individuals could become influential ambassadors for his products. Much like modern influencer marketing strategies, Parson provided fiscal incentives in the form of discounts or cash rewards. His annual "painters' party" served as a brilliant customer appreciation event, enhancing his rapport with this crucial customer base. This strategic move established KPL as a brand of choice among the people who mattered most: those applying the paint.

Parson's knack for building strategic relationships didn't end there. Architects and larger contractors were also in his purview. He presented them with the value proposition that his paints were of high quality and deserved their patronage. Parson was leveraging a strategy that modern businesses recognize as B2B (business-to-business) marketing, a timeless strategy that continues to play a significant role in modern entrepreneurship.

Realizing the need to facilitate his southern customers better, Parson developed a fourth strategy: opening a sales and distribution branch in the Gasparillo area. This move was a strategic business decision, mirroring present-day practices of understanding and meeting customer needs efficiently. The branch was subsequently moved to

Marabella, where a one-story warehouse was erected, furthering the reach of KPL.

To actualize this vision, Parson enlisted the help of Team Member C, a former Sales Manager and Gasparillo resident. Team Member C's role exemplifies the importance of strategic partnerships, a concept that has become a cornerstone in modern entrepreneurial strategies.

However, behind Parson's visionary leadership was a strong core team. He tapped into his professional network, where former colleagues from British Paints and Berger Paints joined him in the fold of KPL. This strategy reflects modern-day human resource practices of hiring based on trust and proven track records. The first Production Manager, Team Member A, as well as the Credit Controller, Team Member B, were former British Paints employees. Other notable team members included the Chemist and salespersons (both initially from Sissons Paints), legal advisors, advertising and signage experts, as well as the Tinter (initially from British Paints). Together, they formed the nucleus of a highly capable team that would help steer KPL to greater heights.

Despite these innovative strategies, KPL's journey was not without its obstacles. The company was up against three well-established brands. To convince hardware stores, painters, and consumers to trust his brand was a major challenge. But Parson had an ace up his sleeve. He offered consignments to customers, particularly those in South Trinidad. This approach, like modern-day strategies of offering trial periods or samples, allowed customers to experience the quality of KPL products firsthand. It was this customer-centric approach that helped KPL gradually earn a place in Trinidad's hardware stores and the hearts of painters, contractors, and homeowners alike.

Stephen understood the importance of maintaining a vibrant and consistent presence in the market. He employed strategies such as participating in annual trade shows and using a variety of media outlets for advertising, including cinema ads, billboards, and newspaper advertisements. His approach mirrors the multi-channel marketing strategies employed by many successful modern-day entrepreneurs, demonstrating that he was indeed ahead of his time.

He also valued the power of branding and public recognition, evident in his provision of trophies, gifts and signs for hardware stores. This approach fostered a sense of partnership with other businesses, an approach now popular in contemporary business practices. Stephen's intuitive understanding of the benefits of collaboration and co-branding points to his innovative thinking.

Stephen's humility, a by-product of his grounded upbringing, reflected in his leadership style. Despite his accomplishments, he preferred to remain low-key, avoiding ostentatious display of wealth or influence. This humility, often a rarity in today's high-stakes corporate world, was one of the qualities that made him deeply respected among his peers and employees.

Stephen's leadership style was unique and personal. One of the defining aspects of his management approach was his habit of leaving handwritten orders on his employees' desks. These notes, bearing his signature, his precise, stylish handwriting, the date, and a gentle request to "please see SSP," were more than directives; they were a symbol of his hands-on leadership style, his meticulous attention to detail, and his commitment to maintaining a smooth-running operation.

This was reflected in his emphasis on maintenance, ensuring that everything at KPL was clean, tidy, and functional. His management style parallels many aspects of the lean management principles we see in successful businesses today, emphasizing efficiency, attention to detail, and the importance of a well-maintained working environment. His close relationship with his Administrative Manager, who acted as his eyes, ears, and mouthpiece, ensured smooth operations even when Stephen had to step back due to health issues.

Despite his position at the helm of KPL, Stephen remained approachable. The employees' affectionate use of his initials, "SS" or the respectful "SSP," reflects a leader who was both respected and relatable. His style of leadership, combining authority with approachability, is something many present-day leaders aspire to.

Furthermore, Stephen's membership in local industry associations highlights his commitment to engaging with broader industry networks. This aligns with current entrepreneurial practices, where networking and active participation in industry associations are recognized as vital for business growth and success.

Parson's entrepreneurial journey was not without setbacks. But Parson persevered, leveraging his business acumen and the strength of his team to navigate these turbulent waters.

Parson's previous job at British Paints, under the mentorship of an esteemed expert, provided him with essential knowledge in purchasing, logistics, raw materials, and technology suppliers. This unique combination of skills and experiences enabled him to navigate the complex world of paint manufacturing with more ease and agility than his competitors. It's reminiscent of the modern practice of leveraging transferable skills in entrepreneurship.

However, Parson's visionary mindset didn't stop at paint manufacturing. He possessed an uncanny ability to see opportunities where others couldn't. Just like the innovators in today's tech-driven world, Parson envisioned venturing into high-investment, high-tech manufacturing plants, such as aluminum can and balloon manufacturing, for the international market. Although health challenges prevented these ideas from materializing, his foresight demonstrated a keen understanding of potential international markets—a strategy highly relevant in today's globalized business environment.

As a business leader and visionary entrepreneur, Parson was admired for his audacious risk-taking, clear vision, and unwavering commitment to excellence. The year 1984 marked another significant development for KPL when Parson purchased an acre of land next to the existing property for a significant investment. He immediately set to work on a new building to replace the old warehouse and offices. Not unlike modern tech giants who invest heavily in infrastructure and expansion, Parson continually reinvested profits back into his business to drive growth, a testament to his confidence in KPL's potential and his commitment to long-term success.

Stephen Sonny Parson's approach to balancing his business and family responsibilities was unique. Stephen's extended family, particularly his siblings-in-law, were integral to the development of KPL. His brothers-in-law were instrumental in helping lay the physical and metaphorical foundation for the company, later fulfilling the roles of Warehouse Manager as well as Salesmen. Stephen's other brother-in-law took over as the Warehouse Manager, followed by his nephews. Stephen's niece and Monica's cousins also held positions in the Accounting and Administration Departments.

Stephen involved all his children in key managerial roles within KPL, thereby maintaining a strong family influence in the business's leadership. This is a strategy often adopted by family-owned businesses today to ensure continuity and maintain the founding vision. All of Parson's children were involved in departments ranging from finance and accounts to sales and marketing, warehousing, and distribution.

The familial influence in KPL remained strong, with Stephen's children, grandchildren, nieces, and nephews currently serving in various capacities within the company. These transitions showcase Stephen's ability to adapt, a crucial entrepreneurial trait in managing both family and business dynamics. The fact that KPL remains a family-owned business today is a testament to Parson's success in implementing this strategy.

This adaptability also came into play as he battled numerous personal challenges, including a series of heart attacks and battles with medical issues, in his later years. His commitment and resilience were evident in his decision to bring his trustworthy family members into the business, a strategic move that ensured continuity and stability within KPL.

Stephen's life was not devoid of struggle; company and medical issues often presented uphill battles. When Parson passed away in 1991, many predicted the end of KPL. However, most of his team chose to stay back and continue the legacy of this inspiring entrepreneur. After his death, the family Board of Directors, with his former Administrative Manager as the chief spokesperson, faced numerous challenges. However, their resolve to prove doubters wrong embodied Stephen's fighting spirit, and they successfully steered KPL into continued prosperity, a testament to the solid foundation that Parson had built.

Parson's business philosophy was centered on quality and value. He spared no expense to ensure that every can of paint produced by KPL met the highest standards. In a world where many companies invest heavily in marketing campaigns, Parson chose a different path. He believed in investing in the product itself, confident that a superior product would create its own demand. This strategy, which prioritizes product quality over marketing hype, is increasingly valued in today's business world, where consumers are more discerning and demand transparency and quality.

Moreover, Parson was a man of strong values, integrity, and fairness. He demanded the same from his employees, creating an honest and dedicated workforce that was central to KPL's success. His leadership style harkens to the increasingly popular people-first leadership model that prioritizes employee wellbeing and engagement.

In 1992, a year after Parson's untimely demise, KPL diversified into the manufacturing and distribution of automotive paints and products. This move was a testament to Parson's ability to plan for the future and his family's determination to honor his vision. It demonstrated the importance of long-term strategic planning, a lesson as relevant today as it was then.

Parson's decision to begin exporting to the CARICOM region, thereby expanding KPL's customer base, mirrored current strategies of businesses seeking international markets to scale and grow. Stephen Sonny Parson's entrepreneurial strategies were not only effective during his time but also remain strikingly relevant in today's business world. He was indeed a man ahead of his time—a visionary entrepreneur, a skilled businessman, and an inspirational leader. The legacy of Stephen Sonny Parson continues to inspire generations of entrepreneurs, reminding them that with vision, perseverance, and a commitment to quality, anything is possible.

Stephen Sonny Parson was not only a visionary entrepreneur but also a strategic planner who carefully constructed his legacy long before his passing. One of the most compelling examples of his foresight was the establishment by the family Board of Directors of the Samba Brewing and Winery Company in the year 1999. Parson had envisioned this diversification program as a safeguard, an innovative strategy aimed to protect Kaleidoscope Paints Limited (KPL) should the paint industry become exceedingly competitive. This strategic maneuver exhibits a trait found in many successful contemporary entrepreneurs who diversify their investment portfolios to mitigate risks.

Parson's dream of starting a canning plant was high-tech and ambitious but was met with unforeseen challenges. The advent of plastics dramatically changed the packaging landscape, causing many canning plants around the world to suffer. Although the canning plant did not materialize, the inception of Festive Balloons was a testament to Parson's visionary planning. This legacy is a reflection of today's leading entrepreneurs who adapt to changing market conditions and pivot their business models when necessary.

KPL's quest for excellence continued after Parson's passing, as demonstrated by its ISO 9001 certification in 1997. This reflects a contemporary focus on quality management systems and standards, emphasizing continuous improvement and customer satisfaction.

A critical element that contributed to KPL's success and brand recognition was a catchy radio jingle sung by a prominent local singer. This clever marketing move is comparable to today's viral social media campaigns that generate brand awareness.

Parson's policy of separation between family and business matters was a wise move, and this strategy is often recommended in family business advisories today. His mantra of leaving personal matters outside the gate and focusing on work within it has been fundamental to KPL's success.

The life of Stephen Sonny Parson is a testament to the power of vision, determination, and strategic planning. His entrepreneurial journey, full of pioneering moves and adaptable strategies, continues to inspire today's generation of entrepreneurs. Just as he navigated the challenges of his time, his legacy guides those seeking to make their mark in today's business world.

Overview:

Chapter 23 delves into the later years of Stephen Sonny Parson's entrepreneurial journey with Kaleidoscope Paints Limited (KPL) and showcases his innovative strategies and forward-thinking approach. Parson's ability to build strategic relationships, leverage influencer marketing, engage with customers, and invest in his team and product quality are highlighted as key factors in KPL's success. The chapter also explores Parson's foresight in diversification, his commitment to long-term planning, and his legacy as a visionary entrepreneur. This chapter serves as a source of inspiration for entrepreneurs, offering valuable insights and lessons that remain relevant in today's business world.

Key Points:

1. Parson's unconventional strategies, such as incentivizing painters and contractors, building rapport through a 'painters' party,' and targeting architects and larger contractors, reflected a visionary approach to influencer marketing and B2B marketing.
2. The opening of a sales and distribution branch in Gasparillo, later moved to Marabella, demonstrated Parson's focus on meeting customer needs and expanding KPL's reach, mirroring modern practices of customer-centric expansion.
3. Parson's strategic partnerships with former colleagues from British Paints and Berger Paints showcased the importance of hiring based on trust and proven track records, similar to modern HR practices.
4. The consignment approach, offering customers the opportunity to experience the quality of KPL products firsthand, served as a customer-centric strategy and resonates

with contemporary methods of providing trial periods or samples.
5. Parson's emphasis on reinvesting profits back into the business to drive growth paralleled the approach of modern-day companies that prioritize infrastructure and expansion for long-term success.
6. Parson's involvement of his children in key managerial roles within KPL exemplified a family-centered leadership strategy, often employed by successful family-owned businesses today.
7. Parson's commitment to product quality over marketing hype reflected a focus on transparency and customer value, aligning with contemporary consumer demands for high-quality products.
8. The ability to adapt to changing market conditions, such as diversifying into automotive paints and targeting international markets, demonstrated Parson's foresight and agility, crucial traits in today's business environment.
9. Stephen employed multi-channel marketing strategies, such as trade shows, cinema ads, billboards, and newspaper advertisements, showcasing his understanding of the importance of maintaining a vibrant presence in the market.
10. His approach to branding and public recognition fostered partnerships with other businesses, reflecting his innovative thinking and collaborative mindset.
11. Stephen's leadership style was personal and hands-on, as seen through his habit of leaving handwritten orders for employees, reflecting his attention to detail and commitment to a smooth-running operation.
12. Networking and active participation in industry associations are recognized as vital for business growth and success in present-day entrepreneurial practices.

13. Parson's legacy as a strategic planner, his reliance on advisory support, and his separation of personal and business matters highlight the importance of long-term planning, mentorship, and maintaining a professional focus.
14. Stephen's humility and grounded upbringing shaped his leadership style and earned him respect among his peers and employees.
15. Family members played integral roles in the development of KPL, showcasing the strong familial influence in the company.
16. Stephen's ability to adapt was crucial in managing both family and business dynamics, ensuring continuity and stability within KPL.
17. Stephen's resilience and determination were evident in his battle with personal challenges and health issues, and his strategic decisions ensured the smooth operation of KPL.
18. His ability to spot talent and build a committed team laid the foundation for KPL's longevity, reflecting his entrepreneurial acumen.
19. Despite trials and tribulations, Stephen's commitment to his business remained unwavering, and his fighting spirit was carried forward by the family Board of Directors after his passing.

Chapter 24

The Leader in the Trenches: Stephen Sonny Parson's Inspiring Non-Family Employee Relations and Visionary Approach

*"When you're at the end of your rope, tie a knot and hold on." –
Theodore Roosevelt*

When reflecting on Stephen Sonny Parson, the founder of Kaleidoscope Paints Limited (KPL), Trinidad, a quote from the famous author Simon Sinek comes to mind, "A boss has the title, a leader has the people". This saying resonates deeply with the non-family employees who had the privilege of working under Parson's visionary leadership. For these employees, he was a mentor, a confidant, and sometimes a father figure. He was known for his ambition, innovation, pleasant demeanor, exceptional professionalism and most importantly, an unwavering dedication to his employees, traits that won him the respect of his workforce and shaped the culture of Kaleidoscope Paints Limited.

Entering the professional sphere under Parson's aegis was not always a cakewalk. As a hiring manager, Parson was imposing and unique, not because of any ill-temper, but due to the seriousness and the high standards he set for his company. This seriousness mirrored a contemporary recruitment trend known as "rigorous hiring", where leaders ensure only the best, most dedicated individuals join their ranks. Unlike many businesses today that prioritize credentials and experience, Parson sought something more. He had a vision for Kaleidoscope Paints Limited, a vision that extended beyond the bottom line to encompass the people who made his company what it was. He observed how potential hires presented themselves, assessing their thought processes, personality traits, and overall demeanor. He sought individuals who would enhance the image of his company, lending it class and distinction. But this initial intimidation dissolved quickly, as Parson nurtured a balanced work environment where firmness and comfort co-existed. Despite his stringent expectations, he was approachable, creating a safe space for employees to voice their concerns.

When conducting job interviews, Parson exhibited an innate calmness. He was never rough with his candidates or employees. His interview questions were pertinent, focusing on past employment history, reasons for leaving, and prospective aspirations. Like a good chess player, he was careful, deliberate, and strategic in his moves, always observing and analyzing. This approach echoes the modern entrepreneurial strategy of hiring not just based on qualifications and experience, but on personality and fit with company culture.

Working with Stephen wasn't akin to working for a boss, but akin to being part of a large, close-knit family. He created an environment where employees felt valued, nurtured, and equally important to the mission of the company. His belief in treating employees like family is a noteworthy example of the practice of 'emotional intelligence' in leadership, a concept often touted as a crucial part of modern management theory. His ahead-of-time approach to leadership not only nurtured a happy workforce but fostered an atmosphere conducive to innovation and productivity.

His employees fondly remember the familial ambiance of Kaleidoscope Paints Limited. Stephen's propensity to include employees in all aspects of his life, whether at work functions or inviting them to his home, cemented the bond he shared with his staff. Even in the demanding setting of a paint factory, he maintained an open-door policy, becoming a confidant for his employees.

Stephen's unique management style, direct involvement, and attention to detail were reminiscent of 'Servant Leadership', an approach gaining popularity in today's corporate world that emphasizes empathy and collaboration.

The importance Parson placed on professionalism and presentation reflected his anticipation of a more appearance-conscious business world, akin to what we see today in personal branding. He encouraged his employees to dress well, much like a caring father teaching his children about the importance of presentation. This paternal care extended to his enforcement of work ethics. If an employee erred, Parson would address the issue directly yet gently, earning respect through his fair and straightforward approach.

What made Stephen's leadership exceptional was his hands-on approach. The operational intricacies of the paint factory were his forte. Leveraging his experience from British Paints and Berger, he set up the factory differently. Although not computerized initially, Stephen ensured that his team comprised skilled individuals capable of producing precise paint colors just by observing samples. This anecdote resonates with the lean startup model in modern entrepreneurship, which emphasizes utilizing resources efficiently and effectively.

Parson faced tangible business challenges such as securing raw materials for paint production. Yet, he managed to steer his company through these obstacles with innovative solutions. One such solution was computerizing the company, a decision reflecting his foresight and adaptability to technological advancement. Even in the face of adversity, he remained involved with his team, communicating openly, and ensuring his vision for the company remained intact.

Stephen's tenure at Kaleidoscope Paints was marked by personal health challenges, including multiple heart attacks. His employees recall one such incident that occurred during a meeting. Despite these hurdles, Stephen's resolve remained unshaken, a testament to his resilience and commitment. He soldiered on, even ensuring the continuity of his signature sales meetings during his illness, a symbol of his unwavering dedication to his team and the company.

Celebrating successes and appreciating employees were integral to Parson's leadership style. Much like modern CEOs who understand the impact of employee recognition on morale, Parson would lighten the office atmosphere with his jovial nature, even infusing humor at times. Christmas staff parties and celebratory lunches during secretaries' week in April were annual traditions, fostering a sense of camaraderie and mutual respect among the team. Aside from these team events, Parson would motivate his employees by awarding Christmas bonuses based on annual performance. He also introduced a tradition of hosting the Annual Christmas Kaleidoscope Children's Treat for kids, showing his dedication to community engagement and employee happiness.

Stephen's love for children and commitment to supporting his staff in need exemplify his empathetic leadership style, a trait increasingly valued in today's leaders. These initiatives resonate with the modern emphasis on employee engagement and satisfaction as drivers of productivity and organizational success. This leadership style also has echoes in today's performance-based reward systems and the focus on talent management. His vision, though unique and personal, was so inspiring that employees often mused that the company would have been different had he still been around.

Parson's dedication to KPL was unparalleled. Even during periods of debilitating sickness, he made it a point to visit the factory, checking on each employee individually. He prioritized his commitment to his team over his personal well-being, a testament to his passion and dedication. Modern entrepreneurs can take a leaf out of Parson's philosophy, emphasizing the importance of commitment and dedication to their ventures, even in the face of adversity.

Notwithstanding his professional accomplishments, Parson remained grounded. His core values echoed the virtues of punctuality, family values, professionalism, and commitment. Much like modern successful entrepreneurs, he recognized the importance of continual learning and adaptability. He encouraged his employees to stay updated, hone their skills, and put their best foot forward, both professionally and personally.

When it came to maintaining discipline, Parson was firm but fair. He held everyone accountable, mirroring modern practices where leaders establish clear expectations and accountability. In today's business world, accountability is considered a crucial element of a thriving work culture, boosting employee morale, and productivity. Parson was ahead of his time in adopting such practices.

Moreover, Parson's entrepreneurial acumen extended to financial management. Much like savvy business owners today, he understood the importance of having a strong finance team and outsourced an accountant specialized in taxation from England. Furthermore, he entrusted his daughter with managing the Accounts and Finance Department. He was actively involved in decision-making across all departments, signaling the vital role of cross-functional collaboration in successful entrepreneurship.

As an entrepreneur, Stephen's strategies were innovative and impressive. He was a visionary who anticipated market trends and responded with strategies that outmaneuvered his competitors. Despite entering the paint market last, Stephen, with a keen understanding of his customers' needs, introduced a consignment model for hardware stores. This strategy bore resemblance to the 'Customer Development' theory of present-day entrepreneurship, which advocates understanding customer needs and creating products accordingly.

Stephen also encouraged his team to foster demand for Kaleidoscope Paints among end users, creating a need for hardware stores to stock his product. This clever strategy is reminiscent of the 'Demand Pull' marketing strategy widely adopted by businesses today. His unique approach and innovative strategies placed Kaleidoscope Paints Limited on a trajectory of success, earning the brand a significant position in Trinidad's paint industry.

Parson's transformative vision was instrumental in the growth of KPL. From a small, family-oriented business primarily producing paints, it expanded to include automotive, rental, warehousing, and many other companies today. His commitment to his vision echoes the strategic planning and execution seen in successful companies today.

Recognizing the digital wave, Parson ensured his staff learned computer skills as early as 1986, fostering a culture of continual learning and adaptability – values held by many successful entrepreneurs today. As software evolved, employees underwent extensive training, boosting their professional development.

Parson was known for his elegant and beautiful handwriting, symbolizing his attention to detail. In modern times, leaders strive for perfection and precision, a quality that Parson embodied.

Customer relationships and team support were paramount to Parson. He rewarded performance, gave special discounts to painters, and hosted parties for customers and contractors. This approach resonates with current customer relationship management strategies focusing on customer retention and satisfaction.

His involvement in daily operations was hands-on. Whether it was catching latecomers or working on the production floor, Parson was a leader who led by example. Modern business leaders often emphasize the importance of being involved in day-to-day operations to maintain the pulse of the business. Stephen believed in the importance of having people he trusted in key positions. His daughter was involved in the nucleus of the business - the manufacturing of paint, and other family members were integral to his operations in key strategic areas including Accounting and Finance, Sales and Marketing as well as Warehousing and Distribution. This demonstrated his firm belief in trust and reliability as core to business success, a sentiment echoed in contemporary entrepreneurial circles.

Parson placed great emphasis on honesty, transparency, and accountability. These virtues, forming the core of ethical entrepreneurship, remain as relevant today as they were during Parson's time. Parson's leadership style incorporated open communication and regular interactions with his teams. He encouraged feedback, entertained suggestions, and acknowledged the importance of customer satisfaction. These practices align with modern-day strategies that prioritize customer-centric approaches and employee engagement.

He ensured the financial stability of KPL by reinvesting his personal funds during challenging times, showcasing his dedication and financial acumen. It's a lesson in fiscal prudence and risk-taking for aspiring entrepreneurs.

Parson's demise was a dark day for the company. He was loved and respected, and his legacy continues to impact the organizational culture. The respect he commanded extended to his future successors, a testament to his enduring influence.

Despite his demise, Parson's legacy endured in the form of team-building events, including the Annual Christmas Kaleidoscope Children's Treat, by the family Board of Directors.

The sacrifices he made for his "second wife", Kaleidoscope Paints Limited, his profound human touch, his understanding and empathy, the balance he struck between family and work, and his transformative vision demonstrate an entrepreneurial brilliance that was truly ahead of his time. Stephen had an ability to make employees feel as if they were part of a larger family. It is no wonder then that his employees, both past and present, view working at Kaleidoscope Paints as an honor and a privilege and Parson's legacy as a beacon of inspiration, a testament to his enduring influence and his remarkable ability to combine business acumen with a deep understanding of human nature.

Overview:

Chapter 24 sheds light on Parson's remarkable leadership qualities and his impact on the non-familial employees of Kaleidoscope Paints Limited (KPL). Parson's mentorship, professionalism, fair approach, and commitment to his team fostered a culture of respect and excellence. He fostered a familial atmosphere at Kaleidoscope Paints Limited, treating employees as family and creating an environment where they felt valued and nurtured. His entrepreneurial strategies, visionary leadership, emphasis on employee recognition, empathy and understanding, focus on continual learning, financial acumen, and hands-on involvement in operations set an example for modern entrepreneurs seeking to build strong, successful organizations.

Key Points:

1. Parson's imposing yet approachable leadership style set high standards for recruitment, reflecting the trend of "rigorous hiring" in modern entrepreneurship.
2. His emphasis on professionalism and presentation aligned with the importance of personal branding and appearance-conscious business environments.
3. Parson's fair and straightforward approach to addressing issues earned him respect and mirrored contemporary leadership practices of open communication and transparency.
4. He navigated business challenges with innovative solutions, including computerizing the company and adapting to technological advancements.
5. Parson's focus on celebrating successes, fostering camaraderie, and recognizing employees' efforts aligns with modern concepts of employee engagement and satisfaction.

6. His commitment to community engagement and employee happiness showcases his empathetic leadership style, valued in today's leaders.
7. Parson's dedication to his team, even in the face of personal health challenges, exemplifies the importance of commitment and dedication to organizational success.
8. His values of punctuality, family, professionalism, and continual learning resonate with modern entrepreneurs striving for personal and professional growth.
9. Parson's firm yet fair approach to discipline reflects the significance of accountability in building a thriving work culture.
10. His focus on financial management, cross-functional collaboration, strategic planning, and adaptability reflects key aspects of successful entrepreneurship in today's business landscape.
11. Parson's attention to detail, involvement in day-to-day operations, and customer-centric approach resonate with modern business leaders' emphasis on perfection, team involvement, and customer satisfaction.
12. His leadership style, incorporating open communication, transparency, and ethical practices, aligns with contemporary strategies prioritizing customer-centricity and employee engagement.
13. Parson's fiscal prudence and risk-taking demonstrate lessons in financial stability and entrepreneurship for aspiring business owners.
14. His approach of treating employees like family exemplified the practice of emotional intelligence in leadership and collaboration.
15. Stephen's hands-on approach, attention to detail, and open-door policy mirrored the principles of servant leadership and empathy.

16. Stephen's visionary strategies, such as the consignment model for hardware stores, demonstrated his understanding of market needs and mirrored contemporary entrepreneurship's focus on customer development.
17. His encouragement of creating demand for Kaleidoscope Paints among end users reflected the demand pull marketing strategy widely adopted by businesses today.
18. Stephen placed great trust in key individuals, including friends and family members, reflecting his belief in trust and reliability as core elements of business success.
19. The accounts of employees highlight Stephen's ability to combine business acumen with a deep understanding of human nature.
20. His demise left a lasting impact on the organizational culture of KPL, and his legacy endures through team-building events and the continuation of his values by the family Board of Directors.
21. The sacrifices, vision, and transformative leadership demonstrated by Parson continue to inspire and shape the experiences of employees at KPL, highlighting his enduring influence and serve as an inspiration for entrepreneurs worldwide.

Chapter 25

The Community Pillar - Stephen Sonny Parson, Through the Eyes of a Friend, Neighbor, and Member of his Church

"Break forth in song, rejoice, and sing praises." - Psalms 98:4

There is a certain mystique to people who can balance their stern exterior with a benevolent core. Stephen Sonny Parson, a friend, neighbor, and fellow member of the Presbyterian Church, was one such personality. From his first meeting with his future friends, when he still resided on the Eastern Main Road, they found a man who radiated seriousness yet hid a jovial spirit, a spirit that manifested when he moved to their community a year after their first meeting.

From there, their camaraderie flourished, travelling to places like Margarita, Caracas, and Panama. Despite his burgeoning business at Kaleidoscope Paints Limited, Stephen ensured he was at church every Sunday, exhibiting an admirable devotion to his faith. As a past president of the Men's Group in 1968, his name remains engraved on a board in the church hall, a testament to his involvement and dedication.

The entrepreneur in Stephen was not confined within the walls of his paint company. It spilled over into his personal life as well, as he combined his sharp business acumen with a desire to help those around him. As their bonds strengthened, he would often be the first to offer advice or lend a hand, embodying the essence of a true friend. Stephen was successful in creating a boundary between his business and his family life, a balance that many entrepreneurs struggle with even today.

A loving husband and a doting father, Stephen was a family man at heart. His devotion to his wife and children was mirrored by his commitment to his community. He organized yearly Christmas treats for the local children and regularly donated to orphanages. These charitable deeds were not publicity stunts; they were an extension of Stephen's essence, a desire to uplift his community that has been inherited by his children.

In an era where businesses frequently neglect the well-being of their local communities in the pursuit of profits, Stephen was a beacon of hope. He incorporated his faith and moral values into his business strategies, demonstrating that profitability and ethical responsibility can coexist. It's an entrepreneurial strategy that modern businesses could learn from, especially those grappling with the balance between commercial success and societal impact.

Stephen's friends played a pivotal role in his life, standing by him in his triumphs and trials. His resilience, the determination to not let his personal struggles overshadow his duties, was a testament to his mental fortitude, a quality that is inspiring for aspiring entrepreneurs. His untimely demise left a void, not only in their hearts but in the Presbyterian Church, where his legacy lives on, symbolized by the organ he generously contributed to, the Allen Digital Computer Organ System MDS-5.

Stephen was not a man swayed by success. His business thrived, yet his values remained unaltered, and he continued to separate his work from his family life. His astute business strategies did not interfere with his commitments to his community, friends, and family. This ability to separate and balance various aspects of life is a hallmark of a successful entrepreneur and is a testament to Stephen's managerial prowess.

In today's age, where the pace of entrepreneurial growth often blinds people to their origins, Stephen's life serves as an inspiring example. His legacy persists, a beacon of hope, not only in the name engraved on the church's board but in the hearts of those he touched, including his children, who continue his mission. It is an enduring testament to a man who built himself from scratch, rose to remarkable heights, yet remained grounded and dedicated to the well-being of those around him.

Overview:

Chapter 25 explores the multifaceted character of Stephen through the perspective of a friend and community member. Stephen's balance of seriousness and joviality, his commitment to his faith, and his active involvement in the community showcase his benevolence and dedication. He embodied the essence of a true friend, offering advice and support, while also maintaining a clear boundary between his business and family life. Stephen's generosity, charitable deeds, and integration of moral values into his business strategies set an inspiring example for modern entrepreneurs, emphasizing the importance of societal impact alongside commercial success.

Key Points:

1. Stephen's serious yet jovial nature created a unique mystique, forming the foundation of a strong camaraderie with his neighbors.
2. Despite his busy schedule as the founder of Kaleidoscope Paints Limited, Stephen demonstrated unwavering devotion to his faith and active participation in the church community.
3. His involvement in the Men's Group showcased his commitment and dedication, leaving a lasting legacy in the church.
4. Stephen's business acumen extended beyond his company, as he offered advice and assistance to friends, reflecting his role as a true friend.
5. He successfully balanced his business and family life, a challenge many entrepreneurs face, by creating clear boundaries.
6. Stephen's devotion to his family and community was evident in his organization of annual Christmas treats for local children and regular donations to orphanages.

7. His charitable deeds were a genuine reflection of his desire to uplift his community, embodying his core values.
8. Stephen's integration of faith and moral values into his business strategies demonstrated the compatibility of profitability and ethical responsibility, offering lessons for modern businesses.
9. His resilience and mental fortitude in the face of personal struggles serve as an inspiration for aspiring entrepreneurs.
10. Stephen's untimely demise left a void in the community, symbolized by the legacy he left behind at the Presbyterian Church.
11. Stephen's unwavering values and commitment to his community, friends, and family serve as an inspiring example in today's fast-paced entrepreneurial world.
12. His legacy lives on in the hearts of those he touched, including his children, who continue his mission of community upliftment.
13. Stephen's life is a testament to building oneself from scratch, achieving remarkable success, and maintaining dedication to the well-being of others.

Chapter 26

Love, Faith, and Entrepreneurship – The Reverend's Perspective on Stephen Sonny Parson

"You came in the early dawn, And you came in the night." -
Rabindranath Tagore

A few days prior to his passing, Stephen Sonny Parson had walked up the aisle of his church, as the proud father giving away his daughter, in marriage. This joyful occasion of unison and celebration stood in stark contrast to the funeral service held just days later. It was an emotional reminder of the fleeting and unpredictable nature of life, oscillating between celebration and sorrow.

A close friend of Stephen's, referred to as his "younger brother", as well as the Minister of Stephen's church shared these thoughts during the eulogy at Stephen's funeral. Their last conversation, at the nursing home where Stephen resided in his final days, painted a picture of a man whose vigor and spirit had remained undimmed by the passage of time and the challenges of health.

Despite the adversity he faced, Stephen was not a man to be subdued by circumstances. He was brimming with optimism, showing his signature fine sense of humor, and engaging in a vibrant discussion about myriad of topics. This undeterred enthusiasm and zest for life can be likened to the concept of 'resilience' that is highly sought-after in modern entrepreneurial theory. Entrepreneurs today are taught to withstand failures and adversities, continually learn and grow, much like Stephen did throughout his life.

Among the diverse topics that Stephen discussed with his Minister and friend, the subject of his business, Kaleidoscope Paints, inevitably surfaced. Stephen was contemplating his future role as Managing Director when he returned from abroad, where he was due to undergo a health evaluation. His commitment to the company, even in his final days, is reflective of a modern-day entrepreneurial principle called 'dedicated commitment', where entrepreneurs are deeply engrossed and intrinsically committed to their venture. Stephen's life demonstrated that he was, indeed, a man ahead of his time.

Interestingly, Stephen and his Minister also talked about a book by Robert Schuller. Given Schuller's influential writings on leadership, positivity, and the power of possibility thinking, it's plausible that Stephen's leadership style was inspired by these ideals. His exceptional sense of vision and foresight, and his ability to create innovative strategies in the face of challenges, could have been bolstered by Schuller's teachings. This was akin to the 'blue ocean strategy' concept in modern entrepreneurial circles, which encourages entrepreneurs to seek uncontested market spaces and make the competition irrelevant.

The theme of family was interwoven throughout the Minister's account of his final meeting with Stephen. Stephen's profound sense of family was not limited to his immediate family but encompassed the larger Parson clan and his Kaleidoscope family as well. His inclusive sense of family, including the familial bonds with his employees, showed a strong resemblance to the 'tribal leadership' concept, a leadership style that focuses on building a community or tribe within an organization. As such, Stephen was not only an entrepreneur but a tribal leader, fostering a sense of belonging among his employees.

As we delve into the depths of Stephen Sonny Parson's life, we encounter a man with immense entrepreneurial vision, a man who started his journey from humble beginnings, working from a very young age. He spent many years in dedicated service to British Paints and Berger Paints, gaining valuable insights and skills that would later prove instrumental in shaping his future.

Stephen's remarkable entrepreneurial journey began with the establishment of his own company in 1972, Kaleidoscope Paints. The Minister distinctly remembered the day they turned the sod, offering prayers before the construction work started. This ceremonial beginning indicated Stephen's deeply rooted spiritual side, symbolizing his strong belief in divine guidance as he embarked on this ambitious journey. It's a reminder of the principle of 'holistic involvement', where personal beliefs and values are incorporated into one's business practices, a trait revered in modern entrepreneurs.

The Minister also recollected the dedication ceremony he conducted when the original Kaleidoscope Paints building was completed. This accomplishment was not merely the erection of a physical structure; it was the realization of a dream, a vision nurtured and shaped into reality by Stephen, who exemplified the entrepreneurial trait of 'visionary leadership'. He didn't merely dream, he made dreams come true, with vision, hard work, determination, and steadfast perseverance.

Moreover, his entrepreneurial journey was marked by the unequivocal support, inspiration, and active participation of his wife, Monica, and loved ones. His leadership style was thus familial, including the traits of 'servant leadership', a modern leadership approach focusing on the growth and well-being of the community before the self. Kaleidoscope, born out of Stephen's vision, eventually emerged as a leader in its field and a household name throughout Trinidad and the Caribbean.

Apart from being a successful entrepreneur, Stephen was also a faithful member of his church. His loyalty, dedication, generosity, openness, and graciousness characterized his stewardship in the church. This is a reflection of 'ethical entrepreneurship', where individuals integrate their ethical values into their business practices.

Despite suffering from ill-health in the later part of his life, Stephen demonstrated immense courage and faith, embodying the entrepreneurial trait of 'resilience'. He was a fighter, persistently bouncing back from adversities. The foundation of his courage and fighting spirit was his unshakeable faith in God. This echoes the concept of 'spiritual entrepreneurship', where spirituality is interwoven with entrepreneurial ventures to offer a deeper meaning and purpose.

Stephen was not just a businessman; he was a scholar, a thinker, an avid reader. He was interested in religious texts from different faiths, including the Bible and the Bhagavad Gita. His curiosity and respect for diverse religious philosophies mark him as a 'learning entrepreneur', a concept that encourages entrepreneurs to continually learn and grow.

Furthermore, he found strength and inspiration in religious songs, particularly bhajans and other Indian music, showcasing his appreciation for cultural diversity. This aspect of Stephen's personality mirrors the modern entrepreneurial trait of 'cultural intelligence', emphasizing the importance of understanding and respecting diverse cultures in today's globalized business landscape.

Stephen Sonny Parson was a man whose life was filled with the spirit of God and prayer, a man who, in the face of death, was prepared to go home to God. He responsibly made preparations for his loved ones, showcasing his considerate and responsible personality traits, which mirror the concept of 'responsible entrepreneurship'.

Stephen Sonny Parson's life was a tapestry of accomplishments. His diligence and entrepreneurial acumen led to him building an empire, placing his family on a secure financial footing. Despite his swift success, Stephen had a humility that transcended his social standing. Today, modern entrepreneurs strive to balance financial success with societal responsibility, mirroring Stephen's approach.

Beyond his entrepreneurial accomplishments, Stephen's legacy was etched in love and kindness. Known for his gentle and loving nature, his legacy was not just about wealth creation but also about fostering love among those around him. This aligns with the modern-day concept of 'conscious capitalism', where businesses seek to benefit all stakeholders, including employees and the community.

Reflecting on Stephen's health struggles, the Minister reminded us that Stephen's life was extended by almost seven miraculous years, during which he was able to enjoy his grandchildren and continue to guide his company. The very fact that he was given this extension indicates that, much like a seasoned entrepreneur, he was able to navigate challenges and uncertainties. His resilience resonates with the entrepreneurial trait of adaptability, crucial in today's ever-evolving business landscape.

Stephen's fascination with Rabindranath Tagore's writings showcased his inclination towards intellectual stimulation and cultural appreciation. This interest in global literature aligns with the modern entrepreneurial trait of 'global mindset', essential for thriving in today's interconnected world.

Tagore's poems, "Gardener 61: Peace, My Heart," as well as," Crossing 75: Guests of My Life," cherished by Stephen, beautifully encapsulate his journey: from a man building a business empire to a man whose heart was full of love for all. The poem also symbolizes his departure from this world, not as an end but a graceful transition into completeness. This interpretation of life and death mirrors the entrepreneurial trait of 'perspective', seeing opportunities where others see the end.

The concluding lines of Tagore's poetry serve as an apt epitaph for Stephen, illustrating his life as a beacon of light and music that left an everlasting mark on those around him. Stephen's journey was not merely about establishing Kaleidoscope Paints; it was about leaving footprints that would inspire others to tread the path of entrepreneurial success without losing their essence.

Stephen Sonny Parson, indeed, was a unique human being, one of a kind. His journey exhibits traits modern entrepreneurs aspire to: resilience, vision, adaptability, a global mindset, and perspective. His life serves as an enduring reminder that entrepreneurship is not just about building businesses, but about touching lives and leaving an inspiring legacy.

Stephen Sonny Parson, the entrepreneurial maestro of Kaleidoscope Paints, was not just a business mogul but a family man, a visionary, and an inspiring leader who achieved greatness at a young age, the loving husband, the proud father, the faithful friend, and the visionary founder of Kaleidoscope Paints. His life story, as viewed through the eyes of his Minister and friend, pays a tribute and offers valuable insights into his spirit and the human aspect of his leadership. His legacy serves as an inspiration for modern entrepreneurs, proving that success can be achieved without compromising on love, faith, and humanity. His life's journey, filled with unwavering commitment, resilience, visionary thinking, and a deep sense of community, reaffirms the essence of his life mantra - a harmonious blend of business and heart. His life, in many ways, was a beautiful song, one that will continue to reverberate in the annals of entrepreneurship.

Overview:

Chapter 26 provides insight into the spiritual and personal dimensions of Stephen's life as seen through the perspective of his Minister and friend. It explores Stephen's resilience, commitment to his business even in his final days, and his visionary leadership. The chapter delves into Stephen's faith, his incorporation of ethical values into his business practices, and his appreciation for cultural diversity. It also highlights Stephen's responsible and considerate nature, his love for his family and community, and his intellectual curiosity. Through his journey, Stephen exemplifies the traits and values that modern entrepreneurs aspire to, including resilience, adaptability, visionary thinking, a global mindset, and the ability to balance business success with love and humanity.

Key Points:

1. Stephen's undimmed enthusiasm, humor, and vibrant discussions in his final days demonstrate resilience and a zest for life, reflecting the concept of resilience in entrepreneurship.
2. Stephen's commitment to Kaleidoscope Paints, even during his health challenges, embodies the concept of dedicated commitment, where entrepreneurs are deeply involved and intrinsically committed to their ventures.
3. Stephen's interest in Robert Schuller's writings on leadership and possibility thinking likely influenced his visionary leadership and innovative strategies, similar to the concept of the blue ocean strategy in modern entrepreneurship.
4. Stephen's inclusive sense of family and his fostering of a sense of belonging among employees align with the concept of tribal leadership, where leaders build a community or tribe within an organization.

5. Stephen's ability to establish familial bonds with his employees reflects the importance of employee satisfaction and love for a company as emphasized in modern leadership principles.
6. Stephen's early work experience at British Paints and Berger Paints provided valuable insights and skills that shaped his entrepreneurial journey.
7. The ceremonial beginning of Kaleidoscope Paints symbolized Stephen's holistic involvement, incorporating personal beliefs and values into his business practices.
8. The completion of the original Kaleidoscope Paints building represented Stephen's visionary leadership and his ability to turn dreams into reality.
9. Stephen's involvement of his wife, Monica, and loved ones in his business exemplified a familial leadership style and the concept of servant leadership.
10. Stephen's stewardship in the church showcased his loyalty, dedication, generosity, openness, and graciousness, reflecting the integration of ethical values into his business practices.
11. Stephen's resilience and faith in the face of health challenges align with the concept of spiritual entrepreneurship, where spirituality is intertwined with entrepreneurial ventures.
12. Stephen's curiosity, love for learning, and interest in global literature demonstrate the traits of a learning entrepreneur and a global mindset.
13. Stephen's preparation for his loved ones and his responsible personality reflect the concept of responsible entrepreneurship.
14. Stephen's humility, balance between financial success and societal responsibility, and his legacy of love and kindness align with the principles of conscious capitalism.

15. Stephen's ability to navigate challenges and uncertainties demonstrates adaptability, another crucial trait in modern entrepreneurship.
16. Stephen's appreciation for cultural diversity and his interest in religious texts from different faiths embody the concept of cultural intelligence.
17. Stephen's life journey serves as a reminder of the importance of leaving an inspiring legacy that inspires others to follow the path of entrepreneurial success without losing their essence.

CHAPTER 27

A LEADER IN MANY FACETS TO HIS NIECES AND NEPHEWS

"Great things He has taught us, great things He has done."
– Hymn: "To God Be the Glory"

Stephen Sonny Parson, known with affection and respect by his nieces and nephews as an emblematic figure, was more than just an uncle. He was their father figure, their guiding light, someone they revered for his exceptional wisdom, humility, and entrepreneurial prowess. Stephen was not just a tycoon but a benevolent patriarch to his nieces and nephews who were brought up in single-parent homes. His presence was a lodestar that significantly shaped their lives and values. As a prominent businessman and the founder of Kaleidoscope Paints Limited, Stephen Parson influenced not just his family but also the wider community.

His nieces, who worked briefly at Kaleidoscope Paints Limited (KPL), shared tender memories of Parson as a man who donned various roles – uncle, father, husband, grandfather, neighbor, and friend. His overarching love, genuineness, and passion for helping people define his persona, reflecting modern entrepreneurial tenets of social responsibility and empathetic leadership. His actions underscored the importance of considering the broader societal impact of one's endeavors, well before the emergence of conscious capitalism.

Parson's nieces and nephews revered him, a sentiment stemming from their deep admiration and fear. Their fear, ironically, wasn't born of his harshness, but his unequivocal honesty. Parson would tell you the truth, however uncomfortable. Today, this straightforward approach is widely appreciated in entrepreneurship as it fosters trust and transparency, the pillars of a healthy business relationship.

Beyond his entrepreneurial endeavors, Stephen was a man of traditions, cherishing family gatherings and ensuring every birthday was celebrated. He had a unique way of making each birthday special - he would play record music, a family tradition that has been passed down the generations. He knew the importance of working hard and advocated for honesty in all dealings, principles that continue to guide his family and Kaleidoscope Paints Limited.

The childhood of his nieces and nephews was punctuated by memorable drives around Trinidad, frequent riverside trips, visits to the market, and shared indulgence in Indian music. In family gatherings, such as in the heights of Aripo and Lopinot, Stephen was the heart and soul of the occasions. He consistently ensured the inclusion of every family member in these cherished times, thus fostering a strong bond among all. His practice of inclusivity resonated with his entrepreneurial belief of team cohesion, a strategy well-adopted by modern-day entrepreneurs.

Being a visionary entrepreneur, Stephen also demonstrated a remarkable ability to uplift his family and community economically. Despite his nieces' youthful fear of his stern demeanor, he ensured their financial security. His initiative to open businesses for the parents of his nieces and nephews exemplifies his generosity and strategic vision. He offered his family members jobs at Kaleidoscope Paints Limited, emphasizing the importance of familial ties and work ethic. Stephen's act of blending business acumen with his innate desire to improve the conditions of his loved ones mirrored modern entrepreneurial strategies that prioritize social impact, mitigate risk and promote sustainable growth, as well as his forward-thinking strategy of diversifying ventures.

Despite his entrepreneurial success, Parson remained down-to-earth. Parson's heart was a vibrant mosaic of kindness, ambition, and generosity. His annual tradition, the Christmas Kaleidoscope Children's Treat, demonstrated this. He orchestrated grand festivities for hundreds of children in the community and Trinidad as a whole. This community engagement echoes the modern entrepreneurial concept of corporate social responsibility (CSR), reflecting Parson's visionary leadership long before CSR became a recognized business practice. His fondness for children also manifested in a dream to start a balloon business, especially with the similarities in raw materials required, a venture he unfortunately couldn't actualize before his passing.

Stephen would pay for goods in the market he didn't need and buy from roadside vendors, especially children, urging them to keep the produce and expecting nothing in return, just to give them sales. This genuine, philanthropic persona made him a titan not only in business but in life, fostering a supportive community and showing his innate kindness. His benevolence underpins the concept of "giving back," a core tenet of contemporary entrepreneurship.

Parson's fondness for children was also exhibited in his continued support for local orphanages, often visiting, donating, and even cooking dishes for them. His approach to charitable work reflects a socially conscious entrepreneurial mindset, a precursor to the "triple bottom line" approach, considering not just profit, but also social and environmental impacts.

Similarly, his love for Indian classical music, flying, and travels to Europe underpin the modern entrepreneurial belief in the importance of personal growth and embracing global cultures for holistic development.

Parson's entrepreneurial journey wasn't always rosy; he had his share of struggles. From riding a bike, owning one car, and feeding a large family, he eventually built a legacy that has benefited multiple generations. His perseverance and tenacity exemplify the indomitable spirit that is characteristic of many successful entrepreneurs. The resilience he displayed aligns with a modern entrepreneurial narrative: success doesn't come easy; it's the result of hard work, dedication, and unwavering determination.

Stephen never shied away from creating teaching moments. His unique way of imparting financial lessons, such as awarding monetary gifts in return for simple tasks, echoed an approach seen in successful entrepreneurs today. They value hard work, believing that money earned through effort breeds a sense of responsibility and ownership. It's this clever and compassionate strategy that led him to surprise his family members with remarkable gifts, marking rites of passages for them.

His niece recalls dyeing his hair, squeezing his feet, paints a warm picture of Parson as a family man. These instances of humanizing vulnerability deepen the respect for Parson, demonstrating that he was more than a business icon; he was a man of heart.

Stephen's leadership at Kaleidoscope Paints Limited was characterized by sternness and formality. Yet, he maintained an air of fairness and equality, treating all employees as members of an extended family, fostering a nurturing work culture. He consistently prioritized personal interactions, walking around the office, engaging with employees, echoing modern entrepreneurial practices that stress transparency and open communication.

His niece recalls him as a tall, serious, impeccably dressed figure – the epitome of a professional entrepreneur. Parson, radiating responsibility and intelligence, was unmistakable as "The Boss" of KPL. His aura reminded everyone of the importance of personal branding and professional image, emphasizing authenticity, which is a cornerstone of modern entrepreneurial success.

In the annals of Kaleidoscope Paints Limited, there were many intriguing stories about Stephen Sonny Parson, affectionately known as "The Boss". His approach to hiring was as unique as his entrepreneurial spirit. One such anecdote hails from an employee who vividly remembers his job interview with Stephen. This employee took immense pride in his association with the company, even going so far as to call himself a Parson in conversation with other employees. This showcases the close and personal relationship Stephen fostered with his staff, further underscoring his unique approach to leadership and team-building. He recalls being overcome with nerves, unsure about what to say when facing "The Boss". To his surprise, instead of launching straight into the interview, Stephen directed him to sit in a chair and take some time to gather his thoughts, reassuring him that he would return shortly.

This seemingly simple gesture was a testament to Stephen's understanding and compassionate nature. The potential employee spent around 30 minutes ruminating over his responses and reasons for wanting the job. When Stephen returned and saw his contemplative state, he immediately offered him the position. This unusual interviewing technique, encouraging candidates to introspect and consider their responses deeply, speaks volumes about Stephen's insightful leadership style, a testament to his ability to recognize potential and foster growth.

Stephen's patience, generosity, and practical lessons marked him as a transformative leader, ahead of his time. He took time to personally guide his employees, again demonstrating the qualities of modern entrepreneurs who believe in upskilling and mentoring their workforce. His encouragement for his niece to learn shorthand underscores his belief in lifelong learning, a trait widely celebrated in today's entrepreneurial realm.

Stephen's legacy continues to be defined by the values and lessons he instilled in his family and employees. He emphasized honesty, hard work, and the importance of standing by one's word. These principles formed the bedrock of his approach to life and business. The commitment to these values allowed him to balance his family responsibilities, support his wife, Monica, while leading a rapidly expanding enterprise.

A deeply religious man, Parson was a constant presence in church, often seen sitting seriously beside his wife, Monica. Parson was deeply committed to the church, where he often donated paint, participated in events, and contributed to the atmosphere with plants and flowers. This active involvement displays his belief in entrepreneurship being a force for positive change in society. It mirrors the approach of modern entrepreneurs who strive to create a balance between economic growth and societal development. His profound belief in the power of faith resonates with the modern entrepreneurial principle of relying on intrinsic motivation to navigate business challenges. Parson's faith became a guiding light in his life, an example of the resilient spirit needed in entrepreneurship.

As the end neared, Parson displayed incredible foresight, securing jobs for his younger family members at KPL, providing them with a stable future. This insightful act reinforces the modern business principle of succession planning and the importance of securing an organization's future. Tragically, his niece didn't get much time to work under his guidance, as he passed away a few months after she joined KPL. Despite this, the lessons he left behind continue to guide them.

In his final days, Parson's unwavering commitment to KPL was evident. Even during periods of illness, he preferred to stay at work, nurturing his passion project. His dedication aligns with contemporary entrepreneurial wisdom that views businesses as more than profit-generating entities. Parson's legacy reminds us that entrepreneurs are artisans, their businesses, a labor of love.

Family members recount an intimate memory of Parson leaving his home for what would be the last time before being admitted to the hospital. He paused, taking a long, reflective look at the surroundings of his cherished home, as if imbued with a quiet understanding that this would be his final farewell to the familiar grounds. The niece remembered visiting Parson at the hospital. The sight of him lying on the hospital bed, looking as though he was traveling somewhere far, was etched into her memory. His resilient spirit reminds us of the grit and determination that are vital to modern entrepreneurship. In his final moments, his family members recall, Parson recited Psalms 23, an emotional demonstration of his enduring faith and strength.

Even in death, Stephen Sonny Parson united the community. People from all walks of life, including employees of KPL, neighbors, friends, and church members, gathered to bid farewell to a man who had left an indelible mark on their lives. His family also arranged a wake at KPL, allowing employees and acquaintants to pay their last respects, reflecting the profound connections Parson had fostered within his professional circle. His influence on others showcased the importance of emotional intelligence, a contemporary entrepreneurial principle that values empathy and relationship-building.

After Parson's passing, his family endured a period of tumultuous grief. His home turned into a place of mourning filled with people who adored and respected him. Despite the chaos, the family showed a unified front, supporting each other, and especially Parson's wife, Monica, reflecting the importance of resilience and community, values that are integral to entrepreneurial families.

Stephen passed away at a time when his younger family members and employees were just beginning to understand his indomitable spirit and entrepreneurial brilliance. Despite his absence, the impression he left on his family and employees is undeniable. His employees recount tales of his humble beginnings, his battles against larger competitors, and his extraordinary journey to establish Kaleidoscope Paints Limited, instilling awe and inspiration.

As Parson's legacy carried forward, his nieces and nephews reflected on the importance of perseverance. They noted how Parson's untimely death denied him the opportunity to meet his younger grandchildren and great-grandchildren, who would have admired him, showing regret that they wouldn't get the opportunity to meet this iconic figure. Parson's story serves as a testament that with unwavering faith and determination, anything is possible - a core message for aspiring entrepreneurs. Parson left behind a rich tapestry of teachings – to be truthful, genuine, and do your best to help others, even when you're not in a position to. These qualities make Parson a great role model, not just for his family, but for anyone aspiring to make a difference.

Stephen Parson was a man of many parts - a loving family man, a respected community figure, a musical enthusiast, and a visionary entrepreneur. He was an individual who not only created an empire but also nurtured the lives of his extended family. His inclusive approach to family and employees, his penchant for continuous learning, and his emphasis on integrity and hard work continue to echo in the halls of Kaleidoscope Paints Limited.

Stephen Sonny Parson was more than a successful businessman. His journey from humble beginnings to establishing one of the leading paint companies in the Caribbean, his nurturing of his immediate and extended family, and his indomitable spirit are all a testament to his remarkable life. His life story stands as a beacon, demonstrating that with perseverance, innovative thinking, and a strong belief in family and community, one can leave a legacy that transcends time.

Overview:

Chapter 27 delves into the profound influence of Stephen Sonny Parson on his nieces and nephews. Stephen, more than just an uncle, served as a father figure and guiding light in their lives. His wisdom, humility, and entrepreneurial prowess left a noteworthy mark on their upbringing and values. The chapter explores the various roles Stephen played, his impact on his family and the community, and the enduring lessons he imparted. It highlights his leadership qualities, philanthropic endeavors, personal values, and the legacy he left behind.

Key Points:

1. Stephen Sonny Parson served as a father figure and mentor to his nieces and nephews, shaping their lives and values.
2. His genuine love, passion for helping others, and commitment to social responsibility exemplify modern entrepreneurial tenets.
3. Stephen's uncompromising honesty fostered trust and transparency, valued qualities in entrepreneurship.
4. He cherished family traditions, emphasized hard work, honesty, and the importance of family unity, principles that guided both his personal and professional life.
5. Stephen's inclusive approach to family gatherings and his emphasis on team cohesion align with modern entrepreneurial practices.
6. He uplifted his family and community economically through business opportunities, showcasing his generosity and strategic vision.
7. Stephen's philanthropic endeavors, such as the Christmas Kaleidoscope Children's Treat, demonstrated his commitment to corporate social responsibility.

8. His belief in giving back and supporting local orphanages reflect the contemporary entrepreneurial focus on social impact.
9. Stephen's love for music, global travel, and personal growth align with modern entrepreneurial principles of embracing diverse cultures and self-development.
10. His resilience, perseverance, and determination in the face of challenges mirror the indomitable spirit of successful entrepreneurs.
11. Stephen's unique approach to financial lessons, valuing hard work and responsibility, aligns with modern entrepreneurship that promotes a strong work ethic.
12. His genuine, compassionate nature and vulnerability humanized him and deepened the respect for his character.
13. Stephen's leadership at Kaleidoscope Paints Limited emphasized fairness, equality, personal interactions, and open communication, reflecting modern entrepreneurial practices.
14. His commitment to personal branding and professional image highlighted the importance of authenticity in modern entrepreneurship.
15. Stephen's mentorship and encouragement of lifelong learning underscored the value of upskilling and employee development.
16. His legacy is defined by the values he instilled, including honesty, hard work, and commitment to family and business.
17. Stephen's active involvement in the church and community reflects the balance between economic growth and societal development in modern entrepreneurship.
18. His foresight in securing jobs for younger family members at KPL showcases the importance of succession planning and securing the organization's future.

19. Stephen's dedication to KPL, even during periods of illness, exemplifies the entrepreneurial view of businesses as a labor of love and commitment.
20. The impact of Stephen's passing on his family and the community highlights the importance of resilience and community support in entrepreneurship.
21. Stephen's funeral and the unified support from the community demonstrate the profound connections he fostered within his professional circle.
22. Stephen's lasting legacy and teachings emphasize the values of perseverance, genuine compassion, and helping others.
23. His life serves as a testament to the power of unwavering faith, determination, and the potential to leave a lasting legacy.

Chapter 28

A Mentor, Father-in-law, and Visionary: The Life and Legacy of Stephen Sonny Parson

"To learn, you must want to be taught. To want to be taught, you must respect your teacher." – Slinger "Mighty Sparrow" Francisco

The journey with Stephen Sonny Parson began not as an in-law, but as a friend. Introduced through their shared passion for horticulture, the bond grew organically between Stephen and the father of his future son-in-law. This early interaction sowed the seeds of their friendship, leading to numerous visits and in-depth conversations that gifted his future son wisdom on life, akin to attending the school of an experienced sage.

After years of such enriching encounters, Stephen's future son-in-law met his daughter at his business - a meeting that changed both of their lives. As a new family member, this led to an introduction to Stephen in a new light, as a prospective father-in-law and a remarkable entrepreneur.

Living with Stephen was akin to sharing a home with a mentor who happened to be a close friend. This was particularly evident during trips to visit Stephen's sister in South Trinidad, or during our candid chats during daily walks and visits to the market. Stephen's charisma lay in his warmth and humility, rare traits for someone of his standing.

Stephen was also a loving family man. Regular visits to his sister in South Trinidad, whom he fondly referred to as his second mother, showcased his deep-rooted family values. These values, coupled with his integrity, were some of the key aspects that set Stephen apart from his contemporaries.

Stephen's entrepreneurial prowess was unmistakable. As the founder of Kaleidoscope Paints Limited, he was intimately involved in all aspects of his business, especially in the Finance and Accounting Department. This attention to financial prudence resonates with the modern lean startup mentality, emphasizing fiscal responsibility and efficiency. His strategy was clear: maintain a team size that the business could afford, thus ensuring stable employment and adequate remuneration. He even went the extra mile, making sure his sales team had their gasoline needs covered to reach and maintain contact with customers.

An integral part of his business approach was his trust in his family. Placing key family members at the helm of his Laboratory and Production, Finance and Accounting, Warehousing and Distribution as well as Sales and Marketing Departments, he fostered a unique mix of familial trust and professional responsibility. Today, such strategies are frequently seen in successful startups, demonstrating how Stephen was ahead of his time.

Stephen was a far cry from a self-centered tycoon. During his travels, he made it a point to bring back gifts for others, underscoring his genuine nature. His lifestyle was marked by simplicity and humility. He wasn't materialistic; he drove an older vehicle and lived within his means. This modesty extended to his business as well, where he strived to create a comfortable working environment for his employees.

His entrepreneurial mindset was grounded in fairness and integrity. He listened to employee feedback and acted upon it, a practice that is now a staple of modern corporate culture. Stephen's organizational skills were exceptional. From meticulously maintained files to the mechanical upkeep of his business, his attention to detail was second to none.

Outside of business, he was deeply involved in his household chores. Washing dishes, performing yard work, or fixing things around the house were routine for him. This down-to-earth behavior highlighted his belief in leading a balanced life, blurring the line between the Managing Director and the family man.

His children were integral to his business vision. Believing in their potential, he sent them both locally and abroad to learn crucial skills, thereby ensuring that his legacy would endure. This focus on cross-training and staff development, now widely accepted in entrepreneurial strategy, was pioneered by Stephen.

Stephen's death left a void in the company and within the family. Despite the heartbreak, his foresight and meticulous planning ensured that the business carried on. The team, comprising key family members and employees, stepped up to the challenge and continued the journey he had started. This testament to Stephen's foresight is yet another example of his extraordinary entrepreneurial acumen.

Stephen was a strong advocate of business growth and expansion. One year before his passing, he led an ambitious export initiative to other Caribbean islands, bolstering his company's foreign exchange earnings. The fact that he entrusted this responsibility to his family employees, even going so far as to send them to other islands to facilitate exports, speaks volumes about his commitment to family involvement in the business. This strategy mirrors many modern enterprises that leverage family strengths and connections to foster international growth.

Stephen's legacy as a mentor and leader became even more apparent after his passing. His family continued to build upon the solid foundation he had laid, focusing on technological upgrades and improved infrastructure, just as he would have wanted. It's reminiscent of today's businesses that prioritize continuous development and adaptability.

Beyond his entrepreneurial acumen, Stephen was deeply embedded within the San Juan community, employing locals and providing annual Christmas treats for children. He recognized the struggle of his people and sought to alleviate it. His charitable work extended beyond San Juan, contributing to homes and orphanages across Trinidad and Tobago. These acts of kindness echo the increasing importance modern corporations place on social responsibility and community development.

Stephen's foresight in preparing his children for key roles in the company cannot be overstated. He ensured they had the necessary training to ensure the continuation of his standards for the company in his absence, demonstrating an awareness of product quality and resilience that's central to businesses today. His decision to phase out lead from his paints ahead of widespread awareness about its dangers further underlines his futuristic thinking.

His entrepreneurial strategy was well-rounded, extending beyond product quality to the efficient organization of human resources. His understanding of the need for specific skills within his company, gained from his tenure at British Paints, allowed him to build a functional, idle-free team. This hands-on approach reflects modern lean strategies, emphasizing the importance of every team member.

Stephen was a firm believer in the harmony of work and life. Despite his devotion to work, he found time for family vacations in Mayaro and imparted essential life values to his children. His approach aligns with today's focus on work-life balance and the importance of creating well-rounded individuals.

Stephen's entrepreneurial philosophy revolved around fairness, trust, and strong work ethics. He instilled these values in his children through their work experiences at his company. His unwavering belief in pursuing dreams and turning them into reality is a timeless lesson for entrepreneurs and dreamers alike.

As an entrepreneur, Stephen had an inherent ability to adapt. This was evident in his keen understanding of market trends and his relentless pursuit of cost efficiency without compromising product quality. He meticulously evaluated every aspect of his business, from manufacturing processes to packaging, reflecting a strategic cost leadership strategy often seen in successful modern-day businesses.

Stephen's legacy lived beyond him, immortalized in the culture of Kaleidoscope Paints Limited. He had built an organization that valued its employees and treated them fairly, and even after his passing, this culture persevered. His employees, many of whom continue to work at the company, remember him as a charismatic, caring, and inspirational leader.

Finally, despite the pressing demands of his business, Stephen never missed an opportunity to offer sage advice or care for his family. His generosity extended to ensuring his children were taken care of in every way, even ensuring they had a honeymoon and cars after they became married. A testament to his commitment to family and employees, this characteristic illuminates the essence of Stephen as a man who combined the astute business acumen of a savvy entrepreneur with the warm heart of a devoted family man and community leader.

Stephen Sonny Parson was a true visionary, a mentor, and a loved father-in-law. His life, filled with wisdom, integrity, and humility, continues to inspire all who knew him. His entrepreneurial strategies, well ahead of his time, resonate with modern practices, proving that he was indeed a man ahead of his era. His life story serves as an enduring lesson of resilience, honesty, and business acumen, inspiring generations to come. His life serves as a testament to his innovative strategies, which were indeed ahead of his era and continue to echo in today's entrepreneurial practices.

Overview:

Chapter 28 sheds light on the profound impact of Stephen on his family and the wider community. Through the lens of his son-in-law, the chapter explores Stephen's mentorship, business acumen, commitment to family, and community involvement. His entrepreneurial strategies, which encompassed fiscal responsibility, family involvement, employee trust, and market adaptation, were ahead of their time and continue to resonate with contemporary business practices.

Key Points:

1. Stephen's friendship with his future son-in-law's father laid the foundation for a deep bond that evolved.
2. Stephen and his son-in-law also shared a mentor-mentee relationship.
3. His charisma stemmed from his warmth and humility, rare qualities for someone of his stature.
4. Stephen's involvement in Finance and Accounting exemplified his focus on fiscal responsibility and efficiency, akin to the lean startup mentality.
5. Stephen fostered a unique blend of familial trust and professional responsibility by placing key family members in crucial roles, a strategy ahead of its time.
6. His modest lifestyle and dedication to creating a comfortable working environment exemplified fairness, integrity, and care for his employees.
7. Stephen valued employee feedback, acted upon it, and demonstrated exceptional organizational skills and attention to detail.

8. His down-to-earth behavior and involvement in household chores reflected his belief in leading a balanced life as both a Managing Director and a family man.
9. Stephen's deep-rooted family values were evident in his regular visits to his sister and his commitment to his children's training and development.
10. Stephen's foresight and meticulous planning ensured the continuation of his business and family legacy after his passing.
11. He led an export initiative and prioritized technological upgrades and improved infrastructure, aligning with contemporary emphasis on continuous development and adaptability.
12. Stephen's charitable work and commitment to community development mirror the importance modern corporations place on social responsibility.
13. His awareness of product quality and resilience were evident in his training initiatives and phasing out of lead from paints ahead of widespread awareness.
14. Stephen's understanding of the importance of specific skills within his company reflected modern lean strategies and the value of every team member.
15. He emphasized work-life balance, family vacations, and imparting essential life values to his children, aligning with modern principles.
16. Stephen instilled values of fairness, trust, and strong work ethics in his children through their work experiences, inspiring entrepreneurs and dreamers.
17. His strategic cost leadership approach and keen market understanding exemplified adaptability and efficiency in modern-day businesses.

18. Stephen's legacy endured in the culture of Kaleidoscope Paints Limited, with employees remembering him as a charismatic, caring, and inspirational leader.
19. His belief in shared leadership and commitment to fairness highlight modern practices embraced by many corporations.
20. Stephen's generosity extended to his family, exemplifying his commitment to their well-being and embodying the essence of a devoted family man and community leader.
21. His life story serves as an enduring lesson of resilience, honesty, and business acumen, inspiring future generations.

Chapter 29

Stephen Sonny Parson: A Visionary Grandfather

"Fatherlike He tends and spares us; well our feeble frame He knows." – Hymn: "Praise, my soul, the King of Heaven"

Stephen Sonny Parson was more than a successful entrepreneur; he was a familial titan whose legacy vibrantly lives on in the shared memories of his grandchildren. Through these fond narratives, we see a man whose character was marked by a delightful combination of intense dedication to work, a passion for celebration, and a nurturing family spirit. His entrepreneurship journey offers unique insights into a lifestyle that harmoniously combined family and business, a strategy that resonates strongly with modern entrepreneurs aspiring to achieve work-life balance.

Parson was known for his acute seriousness, which complemented his entrepreneurial prowess. His business, Kaleidoscope Paints Limited, was a testament to his work ethic. His meticulous focus on his work echoed contemporary business philosophies, emphasizing efficiency and single-minded dedication. His firm belief in discipline and maintaining a boundary between work and family life draws parallels with modern concepts of maintaining professional and personal boundaries.

Yet, when it came to familial gatherings, Parson was a man who knew how to revel in joy. His favorite pastimes included frequent trips to Tobago, where he stayed at Crown Point Hotel and frequented Store Bay. His penchant for river trips in Lopinot as well as to the heights of Aripo, painted a picture of a man who enjoyed life to the fullest, reflecting his ability to separate work from leisure. These joyous family outings reflect the current understanding of the importance of work-life balance in fostering personal well-being and productivity.

Despite his industrious nature and the health challenges he faced, Stephen never missed an opportunity to revel in the joy and innocence of his grandchildren. Their presence brought a radiant light into his life, filling him with happiness that transcended his struggles. Stephen would often sit with his young grandchildren, his face alight with amusement as he watched them play. Together, they would share meals, their laughter echoing throughout the house and adding a touch of warmth to even the simplest of moments.

Despite his frail health, Stephen couldn't resist the temptation to indulge in typical grandparent-grandchild antics. He would playfully squeeze them and lift them high into the air, his infectious laughter mingling with their gleeful shrieks. Such was his enthusiasm that his grandchildren often quipped about their ability to lift him in return, given his small stature in those days. Stephen's interactions with his grandchildren beautifully encapsulate his unwavering zest for life, his capacity for joy amidst adversity, and his enduring legacy as a family man.

Although his grandchildren remember him as being very serious, they also remember him as deeply caring and supportive. The joy Parson derived from rewarding his grandchildren for their academic achievements illustrates his commitment to nurturing success. This unique blend of sternness and affection speaks to his larger-than-life persona. His ability to create a balance between expectations and rewards can be compared to modern management practices that emphasize the importance of recognitive leadership.

When Parson was not at work, he was a figure of joy and celebration at home. His love for parties and Indian music, his joviality during family gatherings, and his love for creating memorable and grand experiences for his family paint a picture of a man who knew how to enjoy life's pleasures. His generosity during these celebrations, where he ensured a bottle of scotch and champagne on every table, or the lavish spreads at river outings, parallels modern concepts of hosting, where experiences are valued over extravagance.

One such instance was during the preparations for his daughter's wedding, held at their home. Enlisting the help of his son-in-law, they embarked on a spirited project to build tents. Their enthusiasm led to an amusing scenario, as they started erecting bamboo poles every three feet across the yard, effectively transforming it into a makeshift bamboo forest. Once they realized the result of their overly enthusiastic efforts, they wisely decided to engage the services of a professional to correct their well-intentioned but somewhat misguided handiwork.

This amusing anecdote not only highlights Stephen's vivacious spirit and zest for life but also underscores his unyielding enthusiasm to take on challenges, even beyond his comfort zone. His contagious passion and joyful approach to life serve as timeless reminders to modern entrepreneurs about the importance of striking a balance between work and life's delightful moments.

Yet, even in his fun-loving nature, he maintained a strict persona, symbolizing his commitment to principle. He upheld standards and had a "no-nonsense" attitude, expecting others to adhere to the norms he set. This strictness even extended to his work-life boundaries, as he ensured his company was a place for work, not play. This uncompromising approach towards standards mirrors the high expectations often placed on employees in today's corporate culture.

However, Parson's life was not without its share of challenges. He suffered from heart disease, beginning at a young age. Despite this, he displayed an extraordinary resilience, living with the condition for two decades. This resilience, shown in the face of adversity, reflects the determination and perseverance required of entrepreneurs in the modern business world.

Parson's impact extends beyond his business ventures, visible in the improved quality of life and strong family values his grandchildren enjoy. His legacy, preserved in the continued operation of Kaleidoscope Paints Limited and his children's careers within the company, provides a roadmap for his grandchildren and the future generations.

The tale of Stephen Sonny Parson is a vivid tapestry of life and entrepreneurship. He was a man ahead of his time, managing to strike a balance between his work and personal life, while still making significant strides in his industry. His grandchildren's narratives shine a spotlight on the qualities that made Parson a distinctive and admired figure – his work ethic, his family-centric approach, his zest for life, and his resolute nature.

OVERVIEW:

Chapter 29 portrays Stephen Sonny Parson not only as a successful entrepreneur but also as a revered family figure whose legacy lives on through the memories of his grandchildren. The chapter highlights Parson's dedication to work, his love for celebration, and his nurturing family spirit. His ability to harmoniously combine family and business serves as a valuable lesson for modern entrepreneurs striving for work-life balance.

KEY POINTS:

1. Parson's work ethic and dedication to Kaleidoscope Paints Limited exemplify contemporary business philosophies emphasizing efficiency and single-minded dedication.
2. Parson's ability to separate work from leisure and enjoy family gatherings reflects the importance of work-life balance for personal well-being and productivity.
3. His commitment to nurturing success through rewarding academic achievements aligns with modern management practices emphasizing recognitive leadership.
4. Parson's love for parties, enjoyment of life's pleasures, and generosity during celebrations highlight the value of creating memorable experiences and fostering joy within the family.
5. His strictness and adherence to standards reflect the high expectations often placed on employees in modern corporate cultures.
6. Parson's resilience in the face of heart disease exemplifies the determination and perseverance required of entrepreneurs in the modern business world.
7. The lasting impact of Parson's legacy is evident in the improved quality of life and strong family values enjoyed by his grandchildren.

8. The continued operation of Kaleidoscope Paints Limited and the involvement of Parson's children and grandchildren within the company serve as a roadmap for future generations.
9. Parson's unique blend of work ethic, family-centric approach, zest for life, and resolute nature made him a distinctive and admired figure in his time.
10. Parson's life and entrepreneurial journey provide valuable insights into achieving work-life balance and leaving a lasting legacy.

Chapter 30

Echoes of a Legacy: Perspectives of Grandchildren who never met Stephen

"Words of life and beauty, Teach me faith and duty."
- Hymn: "Wonderful Words of Life"

Stephen Sonny Parson left an imprint that transcended his time, shaping the lives of those who knew him and even those who didn't. His grandchildren, who never had the privilege to meet him, still feel the effects of his enduring legacy. A closer look at their experiences, and the entrepreneurial principles that seeped into their upbringing, paints a vivid picture of how profound Stephen's influence truly was.

Raised in the shadow of their grandfather's achievement, the grandchildren of Stephen experienced a high standard of living, their quality of life improved dramatically by the fruits of Stephen's dedication. Even without knowing him personally, they've been shaped by strong family values, instilled by their parents and influenced heavily by Stephen's philosophy. Monica, Stephen's wife, took on the role of the matriarch, nurturing a close-knit family environment in which the virtues of selflessness and generosity echoed those of Stephen.

The unique aspect of their upbringing was the pervasive influence of Kaleidoscope Paints Limited (KPL). It was more than just a business venture founded by their grandfather; it was a physical embodiment of his life's work, a symbol of his enduring legacy. This close proximity to their grandfather's vision allowed them to experience his ethos firsthand. The management of KPL, driven strongly by familial influence, reflected Stephen's principles of kindness, hard work, and community service.

KPL became a second home for Stephen's grandchildren. They grew up within its walls, absorbing the entrepreneurial environment. This exposure has greatly influenced their life paths, with many of them showing an entrepreneurial spirit similar to their grandfather, and even pursuing careers in fields that Stephen himself dreamt of, such as medicine.

The tangible legacy of KPL was not just about the entrepreneurial spirit it instilled. It also provided the younger generations of the Parson family with job opportunities, helping to maintain and promote Stephen's legacy. This opportunity, though indirect, was a manifestation of Stephen's unwavering care for his family.

These personal echoes of Stephen's legacy are paired with enduring family rituals. Annual family prayers, blessings, Mother's Day celebrations, and the gathering of family on public holidays and significant dates reflect the importance Stephen placed on family unity and maintaining strong familial bonds. His memory continues to be honored by family through an annual newspaper memorial.

The story of Stephen Sonny Parson lives on through his wife, Monica, who has been the custodian of his legacy. She narrated countless tales of his kindness, his dreams for the family, and his hopes for his legacy. These stories have not changed over time, revealing a man of unyielding selflessness who always put his family first.

The unexpected death of Stephen changed the course of the Parson family. Stephen's personal traits and habits have been passed down to his grandchildren. Some of his grandchildren inherited his love for exquisite items and even his unique hair. In some cases, they carry parts of his name, "Son" from "Sonny" as well as "Stephen", a testament to the profound impact of his legacy. In other grandchildren, Stephen instilled a commitment to quality and profit. Stephen always maintained a high standard for his products, a principle his grandchildren uphold amidst pressure to cut corners. Stephen's belief that "quality is an expensive thing" echoes the contemporary business mantra of prioritizing quality over quantity to build a strong brand and customer loyalty.

The grandchildren also adopted Stephen's steadfast integrity, as reflected in his business dealings. Stephen would never accept a deal at a loss, always ready to walk away from unfavorable terms. This strategy, still paramount in today's cutthroat business world, showcases Stephen's enduring wisdom. In assessing Stephen Sonny Parson's life and legacy, his grandchildren underscore key attributes of integrity, dedication, and the strength to walk away from unfavorable deals.

Mirroring Stephen's firm leadership, one of his grandsons has even reimagined KPL as a regiment, even painting the building olive green to symbolize this transition. Modern leadership theories affirm the effectiveness of such a disciplined approach in achieving business objectives, another area where Stephen's strategies were prescient.

Yet, for all their inherited traits and the enriched upbringing, Stephen's grandchildren express a wish to have known him personally. They feel a certain sadness and envy for those who had the chance to learn directly from Stephen. His absence is especially felt when they pass his photos at KPL, which inspire them with his relentless pursuit of his dreams. If their grandfather were still alive today, the grandchildren paint a vivid picture of a utopian world where every grandchild would have a home in the best communities. But, they warn, this protection might have led to complacency and a sense of entitlement among the grandchildren. Modern entrepreneurship stresses the importance of fostering self-reliance and an independent spirit. It is a stark reminder that in business, as in life, adversity often cultivates resilience and innovation.

While Stephen's direct business strategies were not largely discussed in family narratives, the entrepreneurial spirit and principles that underpinned his actions were implicit in the stories. Stephen was a paragon of self-reliance. The stories of him maintaining a tight budget, exemplified in the same meals of "dhal and rice," together with any vegetable grown by his family, thrice a day, are a testament to his resourcefulness and frugality. They are reminiscent of modern-day frugal innovators who make the most of scarce resources. This is a crucial trait of successful entrepreneurs, as they often have to start with little and make it stretch far. Moreover, his enduring hardships early in life may have informed his resilient, "no-nonsense" approach to business. These experiences fostered a robust personality that proved crucial to the difficult initial stages of starting his own venture.

Stephen Sonny Parson was a man who took risks, who was fearless in the face of adversity, and who built a successful company from scratch. His story serves as a beacon of courage for his grandchildren and all those who hear his story. He demonstrated that life is what you make of it, that it is about the perspective you choose to take. It's a lesson in being brave, in taking risks, and in the rewards that come from doing so.

Just as the toughest part of any building is laying its foundation, so too is the most challenging aspect of entrepreneurship: the establishment phase. This is when the business is still unsteady, vulnerable to market fluctuations, and struggling for recognition. Stephen helmed this challenging phase with steely determination, ensuring that Kaleidoscope Paints Limited stood firm amid these turbulent times. His discipline and strict approach, making a clear distinction between personal and professional life, were likely critical factors in the company's survival and eventual prosperity.

The fundamental principles upon which Stephen built his company were so robust that they have sustained the business for over three decades after his passing. His foresight, meticulous planning, and relentless drive laid a foundation so strong that even faced with obstacles, the company would endure. This highlights the importance of building a strong foundation, a concept that successful modern entrepreneurs continually emphasize.

Stephen Sonny Parson's impact was such that his grandchildren feel a strong connection to him through the company, so much so that they are dedicated to preserving its legacy. From humble beginnings with his first batch of black paint, Stephen's legacy has rippled through time, demonstrating the lasting influence of his entrepreneurial vision. His dedication to his work, even in the face of immense personal responsibilities, resonates with today's entrepreneurs who often juggle multiple roles and responsibilities.

His hardline approach and dedication to his business, however, were balanced by a commitment to his family. Despite the demands of his work, he found time for family outings and special moments with his wife. His ability to separate business and family, yet intertwine them in a way that benefited both, was a testament to his brilliance. It's a strategy that resonates with modern entrepreneurs who seek a work-life balance while building successful ventures. His grandchildren also credit his excellent time management skills for his ability to balance his personal and professional lives.

Stephen Sonny Parson was not just a successful entrepreneur; he was a visionary who left an enduring legacy. Stephen's life story offers an invaluable lesson: hard work, sacrifice, and vision can elevate a person beyond their circumstances. However, imparting these values to future generations requires ongoing effort and a strong sense of purpose. Stephen Sonny Parson, the remarkable entrepreneur and visionary, remains a beacon of inspiration, proving that brilliance often thrives amid adversity. His story continues to shape the lives of his descendants, a testament to his indomitable spirit and a blueprint for the entrepreneurs of tomorrow.

Overview:

Chapter 30 explores the profound impact of Stephen Sonny Parson on his grandchildren, even though they never had the opportunity to meet him. Despite the absence of a personal connection, Stephen's entrepreneurial principles and values have shaped their lives. The chapter delves into the grandchildren's experiences, their upbringing influenced by Stephen's legacy, and their admiration for his unwavering commitment to family and business. It underscores the lasting imprint of Stephen's vision and the continued preservation of his legacy by his grandchildren.

Key Points:

1. The grandchildren of Stephen Sonny Parson were raised with a high standard of living and strong family values influenced by their parents and Stephen's philosophy.
2. The pervasive influence of Kaleidoscope Paints Limited (KPL) provided the grandchildren with firsthand experience of their grandfather's ethos, including kindness, hard work, and community service.
3. Growing up within KPL's walls, the grandchildren absorbed the entrepreneurial environment, fostering an entrepreneurial spirit and even pursuing careers aligned with Stephen's dreams.
4. KPL not only instilled an entrepreneurial spirit but also provided job opportunities, maintaining and promoting Stephen's legacy.
5. Family rituals and traditions emphasized by the grandchildren, such as annual prayers, celebrations, and gatherings, reflected Stephen's values of family unity and community involvement.

6. Monica, Stephen's wife, played a pivotal role in preserving his legacy and passed down stories of his kindness, dreams for the family, and selflessness.
7. The grandchildren inherited traits and values from Stephen, including love for quality, integrity in business dealings, and a disciplined approach to leadership.
8. The grandsons' reminiscence of KPL as a regiment symbolizes the disciplined leadership Stephen exemplified, aligning with modern leadership theories.
9. The grandchildren express a sense of longing for a personal connection with Stephen and acknowledge the importance of resilience and self-reliance in entrepreneurship.
10. Stephen's resourcefulness, frugality, and resilient approach to business, as reflected in his tight budget and enduring hardships, influenced his grandchildren's entrepreneurial mindset.
11. Stephen's story serves as a beacon of courage, inspiring his grandchildren to take risks, embrace challenges, and reap the rewards.
12. Stephen's discipline, strict approach, and ability to separate and balance personal and professional life were critical factors in the survival and prosperity of KPL.
13. The enduring principles on which Stephen built his company have sustained its success, emphasizing the importance of building a strong foundation in entrepreneurship.
14. Stephen's dedication to his family and his ability to intertwine business and family life served as a model for work-life balance for his grandchildren.
15. Stephen's lasting legacy and his ability to inspire future generations showcase his brilliance as an entrepreneur and visionary.

Epilogue

Stephen Sonny Parson's Legacy – Half A Century of Kaleidoscope Paints Limited

"I can endure all these things through the power of the one who gives me strength." - Philippians 4:13

The celebration of the 50th anniversary of Kaleidoscope Paints Limited is not just a commemoration of a remarkable business achievement. It is a testament to the enduring vision of a man whose entrepreneurial genius continues to echo through the corridors of the company he founded: Stephen Sonny Parson.

Stephen Sonny Parson's entrepreneurial journey paints a kaleidoscopic picture, vivid with courage, innovation, and unyielding determination. From humble beginnings in the Eastern Main Road, Trinidad to becoming the founder of the first, 100% locally owned, paint manufacturing company and one of the most prominent in the Caribbean.

Stephen Sonny Parson's journey was a remarkable testament to his entrepreneurial prowess, unwavering determination, and commitment to community and family. His life story, soaked in vibrancy much like the paints his company produced, provides a compelling model of personal resilience, ambition, devotion, responsibility and business acumen, illustrating how sheer perseverance, combined with innovative vision, can transform a dream into a resounding success. This pioneering venture wasn't merely a testament to Parson's business acumen, but also his ardent belief in contributing to the economic development of his nation, at a time when the country was transitioning from its newfound independence, and even before becoming a republic.

Pioneering the entrepreneurial landscape of the region, Kaleidoscope Paints Limited established itself as one of the earliest businesses in Chanka Trace, Trinidad. The birth of Kaleidoscope Paints Limited is a story of labor, love, and the strength of a shared vision. The paint factory, located in San Juan, was formerly used for the cultivation of rice by Stephen's father, Parsan, in the early 1900s.

Stephen Sonny Parson, the son of an immigrant who came from India at the age of four, followed by the family Board of Directors, propelled Parsan's legacy beyond the confines of Trinidad and Tobago, reaching out to markets in CARICOM, Central America, and South America. The personalized approach to customer relations enabled the company to cultivate deep-rooted relationships with its export customers. These partnerships, fostered and nurtured over many years, significantly contributed to Kaleidoscope's expansive market reach and its enduring legacy.

This convergence of past, present, and future symbolizes Parson's entrepreneurial journey - deeply rooted in his past, yet resolutely forward-looking. The company, borne out of hard work and tireless dedication, symbolized Stephen's indomitable spirit and unwavering belief in his dream. He didn't just create a local business; he established a trailblazing enterprise that broke the status quo and challenged international competition. His hands-on approach, attention to detail, and personal involvement in all aspects of the business reflect entrepreneurial strategies now highly valued in the modern world of start-ups.

Born in the small twin island of Trinidad and Tobago, Kaleidoscope Paints was founded in 1972 by Stephen, a man of vision who wanted to contribute significantly to his nation's industrial growth. Kaleidoscope Paints Limited was the first 100% locally owned paint manufacturing company in Trinidad and Tobago, which alone speaks to Stephen's pioneering spirit. From its inception, Stephen sowed the seeds of quality and commitment, nourishing the company with his relentless dedication and innate business acumen. As the years rolled on, the company unfurled like a vivid kaleidoscope, expanding its customer base, diversifying its product range, and penetrating new markets. Even as it evolved and grew, quality remained the cornerstone of Kaleidoscope Paints Limited, a reflection of Stephen's relentless pursuit of excellence.

Stephen's tenacity to establish a business amid adversity was extraordinary. He not only secured financial assistance from multiple sources but also boldly combated opposition from established competitors. His visionary approach echoes today's modern entrepreneurship strategies, such as identifying market needs, leveraging personal connections, and innovatively acquiring funds, demonstrating that he was indeed ahead of his time. Stephen's ability to pivot under pressure and his resourcefulness in navigating financial hurdles exemplify the entrepreneurial resilience necessary in today's volatile business environment.

His commitment to developing a prestigious company is also noteworthy. He strived to bring on board distinguished personalities and ensured transparency and integrity in all business dealings, earning him immense respect among his peers and the wider business community. This illustrates how corporate reputation and integrity, key elements in today's business ethics, were vital components of his entrepreneurial strategy, placing him ahead of his contemporaries.

Moreover, his leadership style was inclusive, fostering a strong sense of community and family involvement. This approach not only instilled a strong work ethic within the company but also cultivated a nurturing environment that was crucial to the company's growth and development. His investment in people and his belief in shared success are now seen as hallmarks of modern entrepreneurial leadership, further cementing his legacy as a forward-thinking business pioneer.

Rewinding to the 1970s, a time when Kaleidoscope was only just carving out its space in the market, Parson demonstrated an understanding of demand creation that was both simple and revolutionary. With no existing demand for the brand, he made the astute decision to "embrace the painters," incentivizing homeowners to paint their homes with Kaleidoscope Paints products. This cultivated a demand cycle, as re-painting would inevitably lead to repeat purchases. Today, this customer loyalty strategy is heralded as a pillar of modern business, but Parson had already mastered it four decades ago.

By the 1980s, the company had become a tight-knit team of dedicated professionals. Over the years, the Accounting and Finance Department grew from a small group of ten employees into a larger office. Parson's strategic investment in scaling the business was evident with the company's expansion into multiple factories and warehouses. The success of any company surviving for half a century in a fiercely competitive environment is laudable. Still, prospering and growing as Kaleidoscope has done is extraordinary. It is a testament to Parson's adept business acumen, which continues to inspire the team today.

The 1990s proved to be a defining era for Kaleidoscope Paints, marked by periods of intense growth and diversification. It is here that the true resilience of the company shone through, particularly during the dark period of the 1990 coup d'état attempt in Trinidad. However, this era was abruptly catapulted by the sudden, unfortunate passing of Parson in 1991. Despite the potential for a loss of direction, the family Board of Directors took the reins. They demonstrated remarkable leadership, steering the business towards further growth and profitability, as envisaged by Stephen Sonny Parson. In the year 1992, the Festive Balloons Company was initiated, and truck refinishes, as well as an 880-colourbank custom-tinted color system were added to KPL's repertoire. These displayed the hallmark adaptability and innovation that Stephen embodied, amplifying the company's offerings and solidifying its position in the market.

In 1993, KPL added an automotive paint division, acquiring licensing agreements with PPG Automotive Paints, MaxMeyer Automotive Paints and Polyval Industrial Coatings. In 1995, the demand for KPL's products both locally and regionally necessitated an expansion of its facilities, resulting in a multi-million-dollar project that tripled the company's daily productive capacity from seven thousand (7,000) gallons to twenty-one thousand (21,000) gallons. Kaleidoscope Properties Limited was also established during 1995, representing the consolidation of property and real estate holdings into a separate division. Kaleidoscope Paints Limited also became fully computerized during the 1990s, transitioning from manual accounting and invoicing.

Fast forward to the 21st century, the company sustained its momentum by leveraging advances in information technology, an essential strategy in today's digital age. Kaleidoscope Paints Limited, a 100% family-owned venture, didn't just stop at paint manufacturing. The company manufactures paint products including decorative, architectural, industrial, marine, automotive paints as well as wood stains and varnishes. It extended its operations to various domains, including adhesive manufacturing (wood glues, contact cement, cement-based wall fillers, putties, body filler, industrial adhesives for labels and cartons, silicones, and caulks), beverage products (beers, malts, juices, soft drinks, and stouts), commercial property rentals, transport and equipment rentals, and even party supplies, decorations and balloons. This diversification strategy, now widely recognized as a key to business resilience, had already been envisioned by Parson, highlighting his entrepreneurial prescience. Today's entrepreneurial landscape is marked by businesses seeking diverse revenue streams, a strategy Parson had embraced decades prior.

This period witnessed the initiation of several projects including the Samba Brewing Company and Winery (established in 1999) as well as the expansion into trucking and transport, Ring Power Rentals (established in 2006), and adhesives through acquisitions of Hanco Industries Limited (Hanco) and Handy Adhesive Solutions Limited (HADSL) (acquired in 2012), as well as the Kolor Expressions color shop initiative (launched in 2013.

In the midst of the economic and health tumult caused by the Coronavirus 2019 (COVID-19) pandemic, KPL showcased remarkable resilience and perseverance, establishing the Caribbean Co-packers and Brewers Company in 2020 and overcoming the hurdles of modern obstacles. This foray into a myriad of sectors reflects the foresight Stephen instilled in his company, mirroring modern strategies of diversifying as well as expanding business horizons through reinvesting, mergers and acquisitions. Such strategic diversification and expansion echo many modern business practices, further underscoring Parson's forward-thinking vision.

As Kaleidoscope marked its golden jubilee, its reputation stretched beyond the borders of Trinidad, gaining international recognition for its high-quality paints and allied products, all offered at competitive prices. Notably, the company's commitment to maintaining excellent and longstanding customer relationships played a critical role in its success. Over these fifty (50) years, the essence of Kaleidoscope's enduring success can be traced back to their unwavering commitment to using only the highest quality European raw material ingredients in their manufacturing processes, and their continuous drive for new product innovations.

Understanding the rapidly evolving demands of paint consumers, architects, and decorators, Kaleidoscope's innovation was once again underscored with the development of the iKolor App in 2019. This ground-breaking tool offered users an array of features, including color charts, the ability to visualize rooms or buildings with chosen colors, and even a budgeted estimate. Moreover, it offered the convenience of on-demand instant purchase - all accessible via a mobile smartphone. The iKolor App perfectly embodied Kaleidoscope's commitment to stay ahead of the curve, meeting the changing needs of its consumers with technology and innovation at the forefront.

As we look back over these five (5) decades, we recognize the incredible journey Parson began and marvel at the resilience and growth of the company he built. Today, Kaleidoscope is a resounding name in the paint industry of the Caribbean region. Its products grace the landscapes of Antigua and Barbuda, Belize, Suriname, Dominica, Guyana, St. Vincent, St. Lucia, Grenada, Barbados, St. Kitts and Nevis, Grenada, Puerto Rico, Jamaica, and Haiti. The company's success is due largely to its commitment to producing quality products and the dedication of its staff, who reflect the values that Stephen held dear. This expansive reach, a testament to Stephen's global entrepreneurial vision, aligns with present-day strategies of multinational expansion in a world growing increasingly interconnected. Under the strategic guidance and the cohesive shared decisions of the family Board of Directors, as well as his two grandsons in key areas including the Accounting and Finance as well as Production Departments, the company continues to establish its presence, demonstrating resilience and adaptability, critical elements for enduring success in today's ever-changing business landscape. Stephen's nieces and nephews are also employed in the Sales and Marketing, Warehousing and Distribution as well as Customer Service Departments of the company to date.

The plant now boasts of state-of-the-art paint manufacturing and filling facilities, which facilitate greater efficiency and increased productivity. All laboratory testing aligns with American Society for Testing and Materials (ASTM) test methods and those of the Caribbean Community Standard for Paints. Since 1997, Kaleidoscope has been ISO 9001 Certified by Société Générale de Surveillance (SGS), one of the world's leading quality auditing firms, attesting to its steadfast commitment to quality, another testament to Stephen's enduring legacy.

Further bolstering the stature of Kaleidoscope Paints Limited is its resolute commitment to offering products and associated services that cater to an expansive array of customer needs. Rooted in the ethos of the company is the unwavering dedication to not only meeting but exceeding customer expectations, addressing both expressed and implicit requirements. A profound understanding of their diverse clientele has shaped their commitment to create products that encapsulate durability, beauty, safety, and aesthetics.

At the helm of this customer-centric approach is the management team of Kaleidoscope as well as the family Board of Directors, whose commitment and vision are directly inherited from Stephen Sonny Parson. They understand the varied needs of their customers and strive to produce paint products that are not just lasting and safe but also enhance the aesthetic value of the spaces they adorn. This approach to customer satisfaction is a hallmark of modern businesses, further evidence of Parson's enduring, forward-thinking legacy. The high standards set by Parson continue to inspire the team to strive for excellence, furthering the brand's position as a leading paint manufacturer.

Kaleidoscope Paints Limited has steadfastly moved towards painting a healthier future with improved low Volatile Organic Compound (VOC) formulations. With the introduction of a new international look, the company unveiled its upgraded product line. Among these, the WeatherMasta Latex Emulsion stands out as a 100% acrylic exterior paint, offering a low VOC, low odor solution with an eggshell finish and a gloss level of 5-8. Simultaneously, the 2001 Premium and 2001 Designer Whites offer a flat finish, an improved formulation with gloss levels 0-4, all while maintaining the low VOC and low odor characteristics.

Not to be outdone, the Silk Sheen Latex Emulsion takes the sheen up a notch, providing a satin finish with an improved gloss and gloss level of 15-25. The 2000 Weatherproof Gloss Enamel, on the other hand, boasts a high gloss finish with a gloss level of 85%. In line with the commitment to the environment, the Supreme Emulsion Latex Emulsion holds the distinction of having zero VOC, along with low odor and a flat finish. Meanwhile, the Supreme Gloss Enamel offers high gloss with gloss levels between 70%-85%. These re-engineered and upgraded formulations reflect the company's commitment to offer the very best, premium quality products, and ensure that the products are well represented for globalized trade, environmentally friendly, and safer for use. The company's water-based products boast a coating that is low VOC and low odor compliant. The gloss coatings have been adjusted to provide a superior high gloss finish with impressive protection and durable properties.

The company also redesigned labels to highlight the added benefits and new features, aiding customers' ease of purchase. The labels now show a product photo, bilingual text, VOC levels, premium product guarantees, special features and symbols, gloss levels, finish types, general product code, the high quality European raw material suppliers, chemical composition, compliance statement, and the ISO 9001:2015 certification. In every step, the company hopes that these improvements demonstrate an unwavering commitment to the provision of high quality products, customer service, preserving good health as well as continual improvement.

Despite his success, Stephen's primary aim was never to amass wealth, but to create a legacy. In the early years, to conserve funds for his fledgling venture, Stephen did not draw a salary. Even as late as 1986, a mere five (5) years before his untimely passing, he was receiving only a modest salary. Today, Kaleidoscope Paints Limited stands not just as a testament to Stephen's entrepreneurial prowess but also to his values of hard work, integrity, and community. His decisions to forgo personal gain in favor of bolstering the business exemplify the deep commitment he had towards his company. His life story continues to inspire future generations of entrepreneurs, demonstrating that the journey to success, though often fraught with challenges, is one worth undertaking with passion, dedication, and a sense of purpose.

Stephen Sonny Parson was a titan, an everyday man whose extraordinary journey was carved by relentless resilience, boundless ambition, and a deeply rooted sense of responsibility. His tale, richly textured and beautifully human, continues to inspire, teaching us the true value of dreams, perseverance, and the enduring power of the human spirit.

Today, as we celebrate the 50th anniversary of Kaleidoscope Paints Limited, we remember Stephen Sonny Parson. His story is one of a remarkable individual who started from humble beginnings and, through hard work and determination, built a legacy that extends beyond his lifetime. His life's narrative is an enduring testament to the strength of human spirit and the potential within us all to dream, to dare, and to shape our own destiny.

This 50th anniversary celebration is not just a testament to Kaleidoscope Paints Limited's endurance; it is a tribute to Stephen Sonny Parson. As we reflect on Stephen's life, we are reminded of the timeless values he espoused, and how, through a combination of grit, sacrifice, and love, an ordinary man can lead an extraordinary life. Stephen's legacy reminds us that no matter our beginnings, we can aspire to greatness, make a lasting impact, and paint our own unique canvas of life. Let Stephen Sonny Parson's life serve as a beacon, guiding us towards ambition, resilience, and the conviction that with hard work, any dream can be realized.

www.ingramcontent.com/pod-product-compliance
Lightning Source LLC
Chambersburg PA
CBHW082105220526
45472CB00009B/2045